"White Knuckle" Speaking

"WHITE KNUCKLE" SPEAKING

▼

Overcoming the *FEAR* of Public Speaking

Andy Ruppanner

Writers Club Press
San Jose New York Lincoln Shanghai

"White Knuckle" Speaking
Overcoming the *FEAR* of Public Speaking

Writers Club Press
an imprint of iUniverse.com, Inc.

For information address:
iUniverse.com, Inc.
5220 S 16th, Ste. 200
Lincoln, NE 68512
www.iuniverse.com

ISBN: 0-595-17018-8

Printed in the United States of America

To my "split-apart". Always with me, always will be.

CONTENTS

▼

INTRODUCTION

▼

During my career as a public speaker, people have frequently asked; "How do you speak so well, without getting nervous? Speaking in front of a group scares me to death! How can you do it?" Anyone can do it, is the response typically given by professional speakers. My answer is; Anyone can do it, *if you know how!*

However, even knowing how, does not make it easy, because speaking in front of a group really does make you nervous. It is an experience feared by most people. Fear of public speaking is the highest rated of top ten fears listed in "The Book of Lists". The fear of public speaking is even listed ahead of the fear of death! Being afraid to speak in front of a group of people is a very real problem that virtually everyone faces at sometime in their life. I wrote this book to help anyone who suffers even a little nervousness when faced with a public speaking situation. But it is designed to specifically assist those of you who are too terrified to overcome your fears to speak in a public situation.

You are, or will be faced with countless speaking situations, including memberships in clubs or associations, the PTA, community or church activities, or at times business situations, where having the skills of public speaking will improve your effectiveness.

Speaker's fear is real and debilitating; therefore it must be dealt with. Having it causes you to avoid situations where you could have contributed your valuable ideas or opinions, which could have helped immensely. If you find yourself speaking to an audience with the stress of speaker's fear wracking your mind and body, you will hide behind the podium and grasp it so tightly that your knuckles will turn white from reduced of blood circulation.

Your lack of speaking skills and knowledge of fear reduction techniques, qualify you for the classification of **"WHITE KNUCKLE SPEAKER"**!

Webster defines white knuckle speaking, or speaker's fear as "*laliophobia*". I call speaker's fear the "**Tiger**", for it is something to be respected and feared, but with enough patience and training, it can be tamed. You have all heard the old adage that sometime you get the "Tiger", and sometimes the "Tiger" gets you. **This book is about, how to get the "Tiger"!**

Knowing how to overcome laliophobia, or speaker's fear is not typically dealt with to any great extent in books on public speaking. There is perhaps a paragraph or chapter dedicated to the subject of speaker's fear, which typically states, "*Being nervous when speaking in front of a group is normal, everybody suffers from speaker's fear*". But there is usually no information of significance to help you, the **"WHITE KNUCKLE SPEAKER"**, who is terrified of public speaking.

This book is written for you, the **"WHITE KNUCKLE SPEAKER"**. It will help you both understand and overcome speaker's fear, so that you will be able to get your "Tiger," before the "Tiger" gets you.

This book is both a "*KNOW HOW*", and a "*CAN DO*" book that addresses solid public speaking fundamentals. It contains new fear reduction and confidence building techniques for you to use to *eliminate* your speaker's fear. You may also use it as a reference book, to benefit from its unique and powerful speech preparation structural information, as well as its many fear reduction techniques. The bottom line is, this book will help you overcome speaker's fear, and improve your speaking effectiveness, every time in the future that you get an opportunity to speak.

"White Knuckle Speaking" is organized into three major sections:

1. **LEARNING ABOUT SPEAKER'S FEAR**
    Learning what causes speaker's fear (the "Tiger") and what techniques can be applied to your next speaking opportunity, to reduce and eliminate your fear or anxiety.

2. **PREPARATION WITH STRUCTURE**
    Learning how to use the most constructive structure ever designed to assist you in developing a "Powerhouse" speech, (I-D-E-A). The I-D-E-A speech development structure both reduces speaker's fear and improves your speaking effectiveness.

3. **FEAR REDUCTION TECHNIQUES**
    Learning how to plan and prepare to use A/V, the room and even the audience as constructive tools to reduce your personal speaking anxiety.

Typically, books written on this type of subject deal with overcoming speaker's fear by focusing on preparation and practice. I fully embrace and agree that those two activities are instrumental in reducing speaker's fear, and vital to a successful speaking engagement.

However, I do not believe that the preparation and practice approaches address the root cause of speaker's fear. Therefore most beginning speakers, no matter how well prepared, remain scared to death and are exposed to failure and personal embarrassment. They are exposed to the "Tiger"!

One final thought before you begin, speaker's fear is a universal problem, so you are not alone in your quest to eliminate it. You have, however, chosen to read this unique book, which is written to assist you become one of the few who will not only master the "Tiger" of speaker's fear within you, but also enable you to experience the joy of successful public speaking.

Ahead of you is not the specter of failure, but the most powerful positive personal feelings you could ever imagine or experience. Successful public speaking provides an emotional rush that I call Speaker's High! Experienced only by a few, it is the antithesis of speaker's fear. When you complete this book and master the techniques suggested throughout, you too will have the skills and tools to experience "Speaker's High!"

▼

PART ONE

LEARNING ABOUT SPEAKER'S FEAR

THE CARE AND FEEDING OF A "TIGER"

CHAPTER 1

---▼---

FEAR IS A FOUR-LETTER WORD!

Riots were shocking America that hot summer in 1968. The nation's population, transfixed to their televisions watched, as the 1968 Democratic National Convention became the centerpiece of National attention.

Against this highly charged backdrop, a young governor from Georgia was selected to introduce Hubert Horatio Humphrey, the distinguished Senior Senator from Minnesota, and Vice-President of the United States, as the Democratic candidate for the Presidency of the United States.

Sensing the historical implications of this moment, for the nation and his own political career, Governor James Earl "Jimmy" Carter approached the convention podium. The convention fell silent, throughout the nation, millions of TV viewers joined with their attention. Destiny was at hand, as Governor Carter began the speech of his lifetime.

Towards the conclusion of his speech Governor Carter was building to the introduction of Senator Humphrey with a crescendo of remarks laden with praise. At the heightened moment of anticipation, to the cheering throng, Governor Carter said: "*...and it is my pleasure to introduce to you the next President of the United States, Hubert Horatio **Hornblower**".*

And you think speaking in front a group is only difficult for you? How could such a dramatic embarrassment occur to an experienced speaker at such a practiced moment? The answer is, the "Tiger" got him! The "Tiger" is the dreaded speaker's fear, the root cause of "White Knuckle Speaking".

The pressure to be effective, and not be embarrassed in this situation, translates into fear, and it potentially affects all who accept the responsibility to be a public speaker. Although your opportunity to speak may not be nearly as pressure charged as that of Jimmy Carter's at the Democratic National Convention, it may feel that way, or worse, to you.

YOU ARE NOT ALONE

The author of "The Book of Lists" found that 41% of those surveyed rated *public speaking* their worst fear, while only 19% rated their worst fear as *death*. The top ten fears as listed in "The Book of Lists", by David Wallechinsky, and Amy Wallace are:

The fear of:
1. Speaking before a group.
2. Heights
3. Insects and bugs
4. Financial problems
5. Deep water
6. Sickness
7. Death
8. Flying
9. Loneliness
10. Dogs

What you can ascertain from these statistics is, that when it comes to public speaking, you are obviously not alone in feelings of nervousness or apprehension that lead to gripping the podium so tight with your hands that you transform into a "White Knuckle Speaker".

TIME magazine quoted famous actor Jimmy Stewart: *"I've never been able to overcome the fear thing."*

In the 1920's noted radio announcer Harry Von Zell introduced then President Herbert Hoover to a national radio audience as *"President Hoobert Heever"*

The "Tiger" of speaker's fear, scientifically named laliophobia, strikes at us all. Actors, announcers, politicians, sports personalities, public speakers, and yes, even you. It can cause misspeak, mental lapses and even physical problems. Your actions when dealing with this phenomena can be called anything from freezing up, to choking, but we all know the feeling well. The challenge is to learn how to handle the "Tiger" when it shows up.

The "Tiger" can come from anywhere at anytime, but mostly he comes from the unknown. That means he is usually ahead of you, where you have not been. It also means that you will not move forward or progress, until you learn about him, where he is, and how to tame him.

THE BIG CHOKE!

For $80,000 at the first Nationally televised LPGA "Skins Game", professional golfer Jan Stephenson, champion of many prior tournaments, was facing a straight, uphill, eight foot putt. It was the final hole of the tournament, and she held a two-stroke lead, needing only to two putt from eight feet to win. After a rigorous inspection of the green, she stepped to the ball, aligned her shot, smoothly moved the club head backward and stubbed the putt only three feet.

As an experienced golfer myself, I have learned it is difficult to putt *"with both hands on my throat"*! The intense pressure placed on Jan Stephenson in this situation was more than she could handle she **choked!**

After sinking the remaining putt for the victory, Jan admitted to a national television audience: *"When I was preparing for that putt, my legs were shaking and my arms were so tight that I could barely move."*

Imagine a seasoned professional, such as Jan Stephenson, under the scrutiny of national television, feeling pressure to the extent, that she could not execute a simple putt, of the type which she had practiced, and successfully completed, many thousands of times before.

This *"fear thing"*, as Jimmy Stewart put it, is there for all of us. Great professionals like Jan Stephenson, Jimmy Stewart, and others must face the "Tiger", as you must. They must also break through the barriers fear erects so they may move on to new plateaus of success and opportunity, as you will.

Sometimes you get the "Tiger", and sometimes the "Tiger" gets you! Is it any wonder that you and I might be a "bit nervous" (or should I say *TERRIFIED!*), when we are asked to give a presentation or speech to a group?

There are many stories of people in all walks of life, who when faced with the stress caused by the intense scrutiny of others, choked. However there are also many examples of others who recognized that pressure for what it was, faced their moment of stress correctly, converted the energies wasted in fear to **power** and emerged the victor for it.

There are two schools of thought of how to reduce speaker's fear, and they both have merit. The first and most basic approach demands that you prepare and practice to a level of personal comfort that eliminates speaker's fear.

Dr. Michael Mescon, renowned author, speaker, and business consultant of Georgia State University, states: *"The best way to avoid stage fright, is to know what you are talking about!"* To overcome speaker's fear, famous UCLA basketball coach John Wooden stated: *"Be honest and be brief!"*

I fully support the need for preparation and practice, however I believe it presumptuous to think that discipline and rote practice will relieve the deep seated fear that the vast majority of potential speakers feel when faced with the terror of speaking in front of a group. I want to help those who are afraid to speak in front of an audience. I want to prevent them from becoming "White Knuckle Speakers".

That's what this book is about. It's more than learning good speaking fundamentals. It's learning to recognize what causes you stress and fear when you are speaking in front of any group. And it's learning to apply anxiety reduction techniques practiced by professional speakers to tame your "Tiger", so that you may emerge victorious from the experience.

WE ARE WHAT WE ARE

There are many books and articles about an individual's developmental years, during which his or her "life tapes" are written. Psychologists believe that the vast majority of your values and beliefs are established between the ages of 3-11, which are referred to as, your "formative years". During that period you learn from those around you and your environment. Throughout your life you modify those values, but the imprint in your mind from those formative years remains a dominant component of your thinking, attitudes and feelings.

Stated simply, you learn most of your values and opinions during those formative years from your parents. Did you ever wonder why Catholic parents have Catholic children, Jewish parents have Jewish children, and not many Catholic parents have Jewish children?

Children are not typically instructed in all of the religions of the world and then given a choice of which they would like to pursue. They follow the lead of their parents who during those important formative years are their dominant influence.

This point was hammered home to me years ago, as I joined Roger, my college roommate for a weekend at his home. The drive there was filled with Roger's praises of his mother's cooking, how much he missed it, and how superior it was to the *"mystery meat"* dinners served at our dorm. My anticipation was heightened for this nirvana of cooking, and the blessed relief from institutional cooking back at the dorm.

Traveling along, I imagined food like my mother made, delicious pot-roast, mashed potatoes, buttery desserts, etc. What a treat this visit would be...and then the moment of truth!

Have you ever had another person's Mom's cooking? **WOWEE!** Lesson learned; I thought all Mom's cooked like mine. Wrong! Roger's Mom did not serve "*mystery meat*"...she served "*mystery meals*"! I was glad to get back to the dorm, for some good wholesome institutional food.

The lesson? You are human, your feelings and emotions are as normal as can be. You know what you know. You are what you are. You are a product of your experiences and your environment. You are comfortable with the known, and uncomfortable with the unknown. It is wonderful to stay within your comfort zone, where you are used to people and things that are familiar, and not threatening to you. You tend not to venture into the unknown, strange situations, or places where you do not understand the environment. You are uncomfortable, at times awkward, fearful and perhaps even embarrassed, when you are outside your comfort zone.

THE GREAT UNKNOWN

Why are you so nervous when you have to speak in front of a group?
Answer—You are afraid!
Reason—Because to stand alone in front of others takes you out of your normal relationships with others and out of your traditional comfort zone.

All of the audience focusing in on you is different than that which you have experienced before. It's intimidating. You are exposed to "THE GREAT UNKNOWN"!

This is the heart of the issue. Since you are what you know, you have a natural fear of the unknown (or what you don't know) this fear leads to apprehension and a natural unwillingness to move forward. A strong inertia builds within you to retreat to your "comfort zone" and not venture forth, said differently, you freeze. When faced with danger, the venerable turtle withdraws into it's shell, where it waits until the danger is passed.

A "TIGER" HUNT

Imagine yourself hiking through a dangerous jungle in India, as daylight rushes towards dark. You are losing confidence in your direction, and are becoming nervous about being trapped in the jungle overnight. You pull your thoughts together, assure yourself that you are in fact on the correct path, and begin walking again at a distinctly faster pace.

A few minutes down the trail, ahead and to the left, you hear a noise. Was it a branch breaking? You freeze. Listening carefully, you think you hear a deep growl. Is it the wind?...Is it a tiger?

If you believe a tiger is ahead of you, you will behave as if it were true, even if it were not. If you were the proverbial turtle, what would you do? Perception is reality!

PARADIGMS

To overcome inertia and venture into the unknown, you must be willing to challenge and change the way you see things. Joel Barker, in his book, Future Edge, describes how you see the world through paradigms.

Paradigms delineate the edge or margin of your beliefs. What is extraordinary is that we as individuals, families, societies, or cultures carry these beliefs as absolutes, while they are truly flexible and change with our experiences.

Geopolitical problems diplomats face in geographies such as Africa, the Middle East, and Central Europe, are perhaps not solvable with currently held paradigms. Solutions that fully understand and accommodate existing deep cultural, ethnic and religious issues (paradigms) are the only ones that will work. And to change what each party "believes in" to one common view is virtually impossible.

Paradigms are analogous to "comfort zones". Operating within your paradigms is more comfortable than operating externally to them. You know what you know, and your aggregate life experiences are recorded within you on your "life tape" so that at any point in time...you are the product of your total knowledge and experiences.

The old adage, "You can't teach an old dog new tricks", has some play here. Acceptance of change was easy when you were a child operating within your parent's influence. Now, as you operate as an adult, you think you know it all. Just a few paragraphs ago you knew there was a "Tiger" ahead…Or was there?

Society and our business environments assume a level of expectation as to how you dress, how you act, and how you do almost everything. Like Catholic parents with Catholic children you operate within cultural behavioral norms that you try to emulate to be accepted in your circle of family and friends. The more you do it, the more you believe it to be true.

STRUCTURE IS A HAVEN

You can improve your skills, and change the way you do things, because they are known commodities. The structure of your beliefs and experiences allow them to be described and dealt with as process improvement actions.

Just as industries re-engineer and change existing processes, you may do the same. Changing what you know is easy compared to dealing with or changing the unknown. There is objectivity and a reality to this process.

Books, such as "Dress for Success", by John T. Molloy, or "Power", by Michael Korda demonstrate advantages to understanding the rules of the game, and participating as expected in our current cultural or business environments to achieve and "win". Writings such as these are both constructive and effective, but the secret in their ability to help, lies in the fact that they deal objectively with your role in relation to the effect of existing structures, such as clothes, room layout, scheduling, etc. Understanding structural situations is an objective process and therefore is relatively easily described and understood.

Speaking in front of a group has a few structural elements, but there is great leverage on you because of the *unstructured* elements.

It is now time to introduce to you, two other words from Webster. The first is deomophobia; the fear of crowds. The second is katagelophobia; the fear of embarrassment and ridicule. It doesn't take a rocket scientist to figure out why these two latent fears can combine with speaker's fear, and create an extraordinary case of nerves in you, the public speaker.

Public speaking is primarily you, alone, on display in front of lots of people. Your audience has a paradigm that you should perform without error, in an effective, professional manner, and you *know* what their paradigm is. The paradigm you hold is that you need to perform in an effective professional manner. You become apprehensive that you may let them down, or do something wrong that will embarrass you. You are becoming apprehensive of the unknown, you are afraid. As this brew of unstructured, emotional drama swirls around within you, you will begin to develop agorophobia; the fear of fears.

Former President Franklin Roosevelt described your plight accurately, when he said: "*The only thing we have to fear is fear itself!*"

DEALING WITH THE UNSTRUCTURED

In the second section of this book, you will learn the **I-D-E-A** structure for developing speeches. You will also learn how to use that structure to reduce speakers' fear and anxiety, and help tame the "Tiger".

Utilizing structure is important, for it will assist in overall anxiety reduction, and ensure effectiveness of your speech. However, it is the unstructured components of speaking that cause the fear.

Many authors and public speakers will suggest that the audience to which you will speak, is on your side, and wants you to succeed. They also state that audience members too, would be nervous in a similar situation and that they are secretly "cheering" for you to succeed.

Nicely written, and fundamentally true, but it doesn't feel that way when you are standing up in front of them. As a matter of fact, you will probably feel that the audience is more than willing to "cut your heart out" on your first miscue. The truth lies somewhere between, but in any case the fact is that when you are out of your comfort zone you feel more nervous than you do while in it.

This is why speakers want to "hide" behind the podium, and reduce their exposure. People hide when they are afraid.

THERE'S "GREEK" IN ALL OF US!

It was speculated by Frederick Elsworthy, a 19th century English philologist: *"That the Greeks may have worn masks while acting to protect themselves from the evil eye of the spectator."*

Nervous speakers hide behind the podium, avoid eye contact, and read their speeches for much the same reason the Greek actors hid behind their masks. **Fear!** Your challenge is accepting that you probably will have some level of fear, when speaking to a group, and so you must focus on understanding it's cause, so that it can be responsibly dealt with.

THREE SUMMARY THOUGHTS:

1. National surveys indicate the fear of public speaking, is the highest ranked fear of all the fears. Therefore you are not alone in your feelings of anxiety and fear when you have the opportunity to speak in front of an audience.

2. Paradigms delineate the margin of our beliefs. If you believe you will suffer speaker's fear, you will.

3. Unstructured situations outside of your comfort zone will cause fear. Structured situations within your comfort zone reduce anxiety and fear.

CHAPTER 2

▼

UNDERSTANDING THE FEAR

IT IS REAL!!

Sir Lawrence Olivier wrote of his premiere performance as Solness in "The Master Builder", "*My courage sank, and with each succeeding minute it became less possible to resist this horror. The audience began giddily to go around.*" What makes this statement have great impact, is that it was written by Sir Laurence at the height of his glorious career, in 1965 while he was performing at the National Theatre of London.

Speakers like actors are uniquely exposed to stage or speakers fright because they are alone in front of many, and they are apprehensive of the outcome. Stephen Aaron is an acting teacher at Julliard who wrote about actors fear in his book "Stage Fright: Its Role in Acting." "*It's aloneness*", he wrote, "*that separates the actor from the concert artist, the opera singer, the ballet dancer. They've got the music, which keeps them company during a performance.*"

Speakers, like actors operate alone in front of a group. Even the most accomplished suffer anxiety or fear as the approach their "performance", which is no different than what you may feel. What *is* different is that they better understand the source of their fear, and employ techniques to help themselves handle it responsibly.

The secret to overcoming speaker's fear lies in fully understanding just why it is you are afraid. The base of that understanding is rooted in learning about your voluntary and involuntary nervous systems.

Understanding them, how they work, and their impact on controlling fear will better assist you in understanding the phenomena of speaker's fear.

There are two parts to your internal nervous system; **voluntary** and **involuntary.** You have control over the voluntary nervous system that allows you to move your muscles, and therefore your body at will. The descriptor "voluntary", comes from the fact that there are times when your nerves obey your direct command, therefore they respond to your wishes and act in a voluntary manner. You do not have direct control over your involuntary nervous system, which is the way it is supposed to be. You involuntary nervous system reacts to external stimulants, such as heat, pain or fear (whether you want it to or not), in a defensive manner.

The crux of what you are after lies within the workings of the involuntary nervous system, and it is adrenaline. Although there are other chemicals involved in the reactive bodily process, the main culprit is adrenaline.

The right amount of adrenaline at the right time stimulates your body to a correct response. For example, if you unwittingly put your hand near a flame or on a hot surface, your involuntary nervous system will swing in to action, produce a "shot" of adrenaline, through a kind of adrenaline "pump", which will assist your arm pull back instantly from potential pain. When your hand is "safe", the adrenaline pump shuts off, and you quickly return to your original state.

The basis for your understanding what causes speaker's fear, and how to better manage it, lies in understanding how to control your adrenaline pump. The more techniques you learn for "pump control", the more you will reduce or eliminate your anxiety and fear.

THE VOLUNTARY NERVOUS SYSTEM

You typically control voluntary nerves very well. If you were at a family reunion picnic, and your ten-year old niece asked you to play jump rope, would you give it a try? Let's say you did. What do you think will cause you to jump when the rope nears your feet? Your voluntary nervous system!

An extraordinary number of mental and physical activities will transpire to get you airborne at the right moment. Neurons in your brain will send electrical signals to the correct muscles, your adrenaline pump will flow faster, your lungs will pick up their pace, muscles will contract, etc. But when it's all said and done, it is simple. You wanted to jump, you planned to jump, and you jumped with the help of your voluntary nervous system.

What do you think would happen if, as you were walking back from jumping rope with your niece, and your twelve-year old nephew sprang from behind a tree and scared you. You would probably "jump" a little differently. Adrenaline, neurons, muscles; all would again be involved...however this time your reaction was *involuntary*.

You would be reacting to an external stimulus. In this case, your body's reaction would have been controlled not by your voluntary nervous system, but by your *involuntary* nervous system.

THE OLYMPICS

If you ever get the opportunity to visit the Olympics, or other athletic competitions, observe the athletes in preparation for their events. Each sport may have different warm up activities, and athletes in the same sport may have differing methods of preparation, but, they all are using their voluntary nervous system to increase the flow of their adrenaline "pump", or metabolic rate in preparation for their upcoming event.

Traditionally referred to as warming up time, it actually is a gradual increase of body processes, directed by the voluntary nervous system and fueled with increased adrenaline that is planned to reach its peak as the athletes commence their event.

As the athletic competition ends, the athlete's brain notifies his or her voluntary nervous system to close down the biological systems it turned on, and after a few minutes the athlete is returned to normal.

The voluntary nervous system is used by your will to ensure your physical and emotional challenges, you choose too meet, are met and resolved to the best of your ability. As long as the challenge is there, and you elect to continue, the voluntary nervous system will oblige, by keeping the "pump" open. When the challenge is gone, or when you elect to stop…the voluntary nervous system will turn off the adrenaline "pump", and quickly bring your body processes back to normal.

Other than forcing yourself to arrive at the location, speaking in public makes little use of your voluntary nervous system, and **therein lays the rub**.

Like an athlete, you should warm up before your speech, and voluntarily increase your adrenaline "pump" to get "up" for the event, and this is a constructive activity, which will assist your speaking effectiveness. However, ahead of you still lies the "Tiger" of speaker's fear, which has the potential of ravaging you, if you do not handle him correctly. He will thoroughly test your involuntary nervous system.

To best understand why you feel nervous and afraid in front of a group, you must focus your learning, on the **involuntary** nervous system. The involuntary nervous system by definition is *not* voluntary, and therefore is *not* controllable by your will. The "Tiger" of speaker's fear has more impact on your involuntary nervous system than you do, this is why your challenge is to learn how to train and control him, in turn controlling yourself.

The involuntary nervous system, through the same biological process as your voluntary nervous system, controls your adrenaline "pump", and the functioning of your related biological (heart, lungs, pores, etc.) reactions.

Two key things are different, in this case, from the prior discussion of the use of the voluntary nervous system.

- First, the invoking of your involuntary nervous system is typically in reaction to an external stimulus (the "Tiger"), and it does not require your knowing intervention to begin.
- Second, and most importantly, without a clear understanding that the cause of the reaction is removed, your adrenaline "pump" will not shut off, and you are in for an exhausting physical and emotional experience.

THE INVOLUNTARY NERVOUS SYSTEM

The involuntary nervous system has two different control systems, to deal with two types of fears; *physical fears* (parasympathetic), and *emotional fears* (sympathetic). These two control systems are designed to balance each other and work together harmoniously as "managers" of your emotions and physical processes. From the influence of whichever system is in control at any point in time, your involuntary nervous system conducts either "parasympathetic" or "sympathetic" reactions. Your understanding of the cause of speaker's fear requires your detailed understanding of the way the involuntary nervous system works.

Your knowledge of how and why your involuntary nervous system works, is the knowledge you need to learn to train your "Tiger", and eliminate your tendency to be a "White Knuckle Speaker".

PHYSICAL FEAR (PARASYMPATHETIC)

You jump when an unexpected noise startles you. Adrenaline flows to make your heart pump faster, your breathing speed increases, many body functions change and operate differently when you are *physically scared*. Parasympathetic actions are the more normally expected involuntary nervous actions (or perhaps better stated as reactions), caused by unexpected physical fear.

For example, you are driving down a neighborhood street when, without warning, a car runs a stop sign and lurches out in front of your car. You step on your brakes and skid to a stop, missing the car by mere inches. How do you feel?

No damage has occurred, and you are relieved that the situation is over. However, if you would take a physical assessment of your pulse or blood pressure at this point you would observe that you are by no means calm.

In reaction to this traumatic event, your parasympathetic nervous system kicked in by shooting adrenaline into your nervous system at the instant you saw the car.

This surge of adrenaline, from your adrenaline "pump", causes your body to change its biological processes rapidly and respond in exactly the same manner as the reactions caused by your voluntary nervous system, (increased heart rate, faster breathing, open pores, widened eyes, muscles at the ready, and so forth.). Because of this dramatic change in your physical capability, caused by fear of crashing, you were able to react more quickly than you could have without it. At this moment of physical fear, your mind drops what it was doing and your full mental and physical capabilities are brought to bear on *what it was* that scared you, and whether or not what it was is removed.

When you discover that the cause of your anxiety is removed, (in the earlier example the car stopped without a crash), your mind signals your body that everything may return to normal, by turning off your adrenaline "pump". Once you know that the cause of your fear has been removed, and your "pump" is turned off, your emotions and internal biological processes will soon calm down and return to their natural state. It is normal to respond to fearful situations with adrenaline driven physical reactions. You will respond with these reactions because they are programmed into your genes, from the fight or flee experiences of your ancestors to dangerous life threatening situations. These responses will serve you well, as they have served your ancestors over time.

EMOTIONAL FEAR (SYMPATHETIC)

I can remember in spite of 40 plus years gone by, my approximately two-mile walk, to our weekly Boy Scout Troop meeting. Leaving my house was no problem, for I was dressed in my uniform, easily feeling twice my 13 years of age, and in possession of my 11 bladed Boy Scout Knife. I would saunter off, down the street, around the corner and on to the meeting.

For good measure, I might even wave at neighbors on porches or in yards, regaled as I was in full manly splendor and swelling with pride. There was nothing that could stop or thwart this Trustworthy, Loyal, Helpful, Friendly, Courteous, Kind, Obedient, Cheerful, Thrifty, Brave, Clean and Reverend future leader of America, as I strode toward my destiny.

Coming home from the meeting was also no problem, until one night as I neared the bushes in front of Old Man Munzenmier's house…I thought I heard a branch snap. The bushes at Old Man Munzenmier's house were never trimmed, and always hung over the sidewalk casting eerie moving shadows in the slightest breeze. And then…a noise. I froze! I just knew someone was going to jump out and get me. I started to sweat, hyperventilate, and did everything else my involuntary nervous system could do to prepare me for flight. And I ran and ran and ran.

From that moment on, walking home from a Scout meeting after dark was never the same, and it was never again *just walking*.

Leaving the scout meeting was no problem, as I would typically have a friend or two to accompany me part of the way home. But when I was alone, the game would change! Boy Scout suit or not, 13 is 13, and dark is dark.

Between home and me remained the challenge of the dreaded Old Man Munzenmier bushes. I never knew then, and I still do not know now, what caused that fateful snap.

Because I was never able to find the cause of my fear, it never ended.

Whenever I approached those bushes I believed I would be hurt and so I suffered emotional anxiety and fear, because of what I didn't know. **My sympathetic nervous system responded to my fear of a *potential* fear.**

Not knowing if there was in fact anyone there, my involuntary nervous system would overwhelm me with the genetic code of my ancestors, and present me with heightened emotion to fight or flee. I easily chose the latter and would run like hell for home!

I remain at a loss as to how to fully describe to you the horrible personal trauma caused by the "snap" at the Munzenmier bushes. But chances are, something similar has also happened, to you, in your life. I know you have each faced your own version of the dreaded Munzenmier bushes. And I believe you probably handled your trauma, in a similar manner as I handled mine.

When you face a public speaking challenge, you will find yourself again in a similar situation. The better your understanding of the cause of your fear, the better your ability to handle the problem so you don't have to run away!

The cause of my running away from another potential "snap", every time I returned home from my scout meetings, is the same phenomena you experience as a "White Knuckle Speaker". I suffered from being afraid of potentially being scared. I experienced the most deadly fear of all, and the very same fear caused by the "Tiger" that traumatizes "White Knuckle Speakers". I experienced **Phobophobia**, the fear of fears.

THE FEAR OF FEARS

Fear is an emotional reaction and it invokes the sympathetic involuntary nervous system. Once more the point to understand here is again is that it is normal to react to fearful situations with adrenaline driven physical reactions. It is also normal to calm down when the cause of your fear is removed.

When you feel building anxiety as you are on the verge of speaking to a group, it is because your sympathetic nervous system is beginning to be active, and your adrenaline pump is starting to increase its output. You experience the same biological reactions as you do with physical fear. However because there is no "seen" cause, as in the case of physical fear, there is no way to recognize what is causing your reaction, and therefore being unsure of the situation you begin to fear what may happen.

You begin to be afraid of being afraid, and you enter the debilitating arena of the fear of fears (Phobophobia). This is where the "Tiger" lives, and it is dangerous territory without the knowledge of how to survive.

Secondly, and most importantly, it is very difficult to end your emotional reaction to the fear of fears, because since you do not know what the specific threat is that is causing your anxiety, it is impossible to ascertain when the threat to you has ended.

Without a signal that the cause of your fear is removed, your unchecked emotions will continue to build until your body starts to "shut down" do to overload. When your body has more adrenaline flowing from your "pump" than it can process, and all of your biological functions are operating at their maximum capability, it will respond with its activity of last resort...your body will close down and you will feint! The physical and emotional symptoms leading to your potential feint are the most difficult to handle, and you become virtually out of control.

Sensing these oncoming feelings you will not proceed further, you will freeze. Being that you are afraid of what may lie ahead or what may happen, that you may feint, that you will be embarrassed, you will do anything in your power to avoid it. **Understanding this phenomena is the key to understanding and overcoming your fear in speaking in front of an audience.**

Look at this process in the context of speaker's fear. Picture yourself sitting in the front row waiting to be introduced. This is when you can hear the "Tiger" start to growl. You start to feel emotional stress and your sympathetic involuntary nervous system begins to kick in to "help" you. It's time to fight or flee to end this situation, but you cannot do either of these, and your adrenaline "runneth" over.

The problem is that in a sympathetic reaction to emotional stress, that has no perceived ending, your internal biological processes begin reactions to your adrenaline "pump", ultimately reaching an extreme point that essentially turns everything you have "on", at full speed.

You become acutely aware of your internal organs or bodily processes functioning abnormally, to the extent that you believe them to be out of control. Your heart may be pumping so hard, and you may be breathing so rapidly that you believe you will feint in front of your audience.

You try to contain these feelings to the best of your ability but without an "all's well" signal, there is no end in sight for this trauma, and your adrenaline pump will keep on flowing. Because you can't control this situation, you cannot fight or you cannot flee, the "Tiger" has you cornered. Faced with no other alternatives to solve the problem, and with the "Tiger" growing stronger, your body goes for the only card it has remaining, you will fear the fear of being sick, or passing out, and you will freeze up or withdraw.

NO STOP SIGN

What is different or abnormal in this situation to most others, is that your involuntary nervous system is looking for a signal to stop the adrenaline flow, but because it is not apparent, you continue until you are afraid of the consequences of your current reaction and not an external cause. You enter a cycle of fear that feeds on itself. You are now in an accelerating pattern of reacting to reacting and you are afraid of personal embarrassment and becoming out of control. You are in a cycle of fear.

Your body, seeing no end and sensing it remains in trouble will call for more adrenaline that will sustain your reaction and not allow it to end as it would in the case of a normal involuntary reaction caused by the parasympathetic nervous system.

You are afraid because you are emotionally reacting to the unknown, and you have no personal experience or techniques to help you bring it to a successful close. This situation is outside of your paradigm, and you begin to fear being embarrassed if you can't control your reactions. You are not only afraid of speaking you are also afraid of embarrassment, and you are afraid of being afraid. You are in a cascading fear sequence. The fear sequence has several incremental steps from beginning to end, but there is one major physical reaction within it, that once experienced, will change your paradigm and remain in your memory bank forever.

That reaction is a horrible feeling in the pit of your stomach that is typically accompanied by a sensation of nausea. You may have experienced this sensation before, because it is the base reaction to fear that foretells losing bowel control and passing out. Although it is a natural sequence of human reaction to fear and panic, it is embarrassing and perhaps humiliating behavior in our contemporary culture and therefore you fear the consequences of continued increasing anxiety and panic.

Odds are, like my experience as a Boy Scout, you have experienced these or similar traumatic feelings or sensations before. When your body moves towards these horrible sensations in a fear cycle, your apprehension is accelerated even more as you begin to fear them too. You have no memory of successful handling of a situation such as this, so you continue to fear your fear and you enter into a cycle of emotional fear without a known end.

The strongest and most debilitating fear is Phobophobia, the fear of fears. Therefore, most people will avoid this situation altogether by electing not to speak to a group. That is the safest way out, but perhaps not the most constructive to your career or your personal development. Avoidance of the situation allows you to stay within your paradigm, in your "comfort zone", and obviously no harm will come to you there.

YOUR COMFORT ZONE

In "A Song of the South", B'rer Rabbit sang, "*Everybody's got a laffin' place....*" He was comfortable in his Briar Patch. You feel comfortable in your psychological "comfort zone".

Most people do not elect to participate as a public speaker because it forces them to leave their comfort zone. Their fear of fear is so strong, as demonstrated by the number one ranking of fear of public speaking, in the book of lists.

However, many people would like to test their own abilities, and enlarge their comfort zone to include public speaking. This desire to expand one's scope is why some choose to try new endeavors such as; parasailing, bungee jumping, or skydiving.

For each of these new endeavors there is anxiety and the first time event. For those who try, there is outstanding personal reward and feelings of exhilaration. Safer to your health, but equally exhilarating is public speaking. For those who voluntarily or involuntarily venture, from their comfort zone into public speaking, the first logical step is to move to the next safe spot, the podium.

As a "White Knuckle Speaker" it's not that you really think that some particular place holds special danger for you. It's just that you are afraid of how you will *potentially* react in certain traumatic situations. You are keenly aware of what happens within your body when it suffers great stress (feeling weak, dizzy, nauseas) that you live in fear that you may "go out of control" in situations with which you may be unable to cope.

Your fear feeds on the belief that you may consequently make a fool of yourself in public. Fear is the most disagreeable emotion you can experience. Is it so inconceivable, that you could be afraid of it for its own sake? Must there always be a cause for fear other than the fear of fear.

There is nothing unusual then about being afraid or nervous or apprehensive when you leave your safety zone. You are welcome to hide behind the podium and grip it tight for all you are worth, for like learning to walk, you will soon let go and pick up speed. This book is about dealing with that moment, handling fear and the fear of fear as it applies to public speaking.

There are four imperatives to managing fear effectively:

FEAR IMPERATIVES

1. *FACE IT!* Do not run away. The "Tiger" will always be out in front somewhere, and you must learn to tame him.

2. *ACCEPT IT!* Do not fight the fact that fear exists. Understanding that palpitations are no more than a temporary upset in the timing of a heartbeat caused by over stimulated nerves, and that the attack always calms down, will help you lose your fear of them. Less fear means less adrenaline and consequently less excitation.

3. *RISE ABOVE IT!* Turn your attention to the way you think, not the way you feel. Come to terms with your anxiety and you feelings will look after themselves. You will learn several effective fear reduction techniques in this book that will allow you to expand your paradigm of speaking comfort and give you the confidence for success.

4. *LET TIME PASS!* Do not be impatient with time. Experience shows people normally accept and deal with approximately 95% of their stresses and withdraw from the final 5%. You may become so paralyzed by thinking about doing, that you put off the actual doing.

5. The 5% challenge of speaker's fear only lasts for about two minutes at the beginning of a speech. Deflection and diffusion techniques will get you through most of it, and the I-D-E-A speech structure, covered later in Chapter 6 will carry you through to the successful end of your presentation.

Dr. Claire Weeks writes in her book," Peace Through Nervous Suffering", "*Peace lies on the other side of panic.*" Withdrawing from panic is your failure. You must lean forward and complete your match with fear. It is illogical to struggle through the vast majority of the trauma, only to stop with the goal in sight.

A favorite quote of mine from an unknown source crystallizes this concept very well:

> "*Upon the plains of hesitation lie the bones of countless thousands, who, on the threshold of victory, sat down to wait, and waiting they died!*"

Don't wait! You can and will do better if you face down the final five percent. Putting the information, ideas and techniques available in this book to use for yourself will not only assist you to improve the next time you speak, but it will also continue to reduce your anxiety at each future speaking opportunity.

THREE SUMMARY THOUGHTS:

1. Speaker's fear is real. The "Tiger" is always lurking somewhere ahead of you. You must tame him to succeed.

2. There are four Imperatives to use in dealing with fear:
   - Face It!
   - Accept It!
   - Rise Above It!
   - Let Time Pass!

3. Using the I-D-E-A structure, speaker's fear is resolved within the last 5% of your effort, which in public speaking is approximately two minutes long. Stick with it!

CHAPTER 3

▼

ADDRESSING THE PROBLEM

Howard Goshorn said: *"The human brain is a wonderful thing. It operates from the moment you are born until the first time you get up to make a speech!"*

Emotional focus is the primary catalyst to a series of internal events that lead to speaker's fear. Emotional focus telegraphs to you that your "Tiger" is entering the room, so you better watch out. The presence of emotional focus is such a significant event that it totally changes your perspective on the situation in which you find yourself.

External emotional changes that impact your ability to control your emotions are powerful and dramatic. Have you ever cried at a ceremony, been moved to tears by beautiful music, or be motivated by a memorable speaker?

The impact from an externally caused emotional experience could be anything on a scale from minor to major. Impacts from fear tend to be on the major end of the continuum. Impacts from the emotional impact of speaker's fear, telegraphed from the intensity of emotional focus from an audience, are approaching lethal. Why else would the fear of public speaking be rated higher than fear of death?

A "SPECIAL" CAMERA

It's time to move this discourse from the theoretical to the practical. To that end, let's skip past speech development at this time, and go directly to the room in which you will speak. I have installed in the room a "special" camera for this exercise that can capture on videotape an audience's emotional focus. Utilizing this technique you will be best able to learn what emotional focus is and its powerful affect on speakers.

Join me in the planned meeting room at one of the national chain hotels near you. The room will accommodate approximately 250 people and it has chairs for the audience set up in rows of ten. It also has a low stage in the front of the room, adorned by a hotel podium.

You are here to assess the emotional dynamics that typically go on in a meeting room causing you, as the speaker, to be nervous. The "camera" is a teaching tool that will help you understand the subject of emotional focus, so let me explain how it works. The "camera" is located on the ceiling, in the center of the room, and has an aerial view of the entire room. The "camera's" view is similar to that of a TV blimp hovering over a sporting event. If people were in the room, you would see the tops of their heads.

The "camera" through which you are looking is special, because it records only visual emotion between people in the room. It does this bit of magic by recording imaginary lines that extend from one person's eyes to other people or objects in the room. Like headlights peering into the darkness from the front of a car, these laser-like lines of emotional focus emanate from each and every person who enters the room.

VISUALIZATION OF FOCUS

Start your camera running when the room is empty and only the room's furniture is visible. The meeting planner arrives first in the room to ensure all of the facilities are ready. As the planner moves about the room two lines radiate from her eyes to different points around the room as she focuses on the stage, podium, light switches, furniture etc. With the help of the "camera", you are able to visualize emotional focus for the first time.

Next the evening's speaker comes in to become familiar with the room and its surroundings. She too has "imaginary lines" emanating from her eyes. The special camera now captures two sets of lines in the room; one set from each party. As they discover each other in the room their eyes meet and the camera observes both sets of lines aligning in a parallel manner as they exchange greetings.

Through the "camera" you can sense an increase in intensity, as their emotional focus aligns. When they look away from each other, the camera observes the two separate sets of emotional focus lines moving about, focusing on objects of importance to their owner. Now your observations indicate a lesser intensity, as their focus dissipates from each other.

As the speaker stands at the front of the room and tests the microphone for proper volume, she asks the meeting planner if she can hear at the back. During the question lines radiate from the speaker to the planner, and while the response is given, two sets of parallel lines connect them once again, and the intensity builds.

Well, now you have the concept of the power of this special camera and how it works on just two people. It is now time for you to use it on an increasing number of people, as the room fills with the evening's audience.

Start the camera, as they begin to arrive. What you will see, from above, is an ever-increasing number of intersecting lines, created by two "head-lights" of focus from each person entering the room. Each person's eyes will be darting randomly about the audience and room until the room is virtually blackened with intersecting lines, in a random pattern.

The focus of the room at this time is *disbursed* randomly among many people and things until the meeting begins to be brought to order.

The evening's moderator moves to the front of the room, the audience takes their seats, and their collective focus begins to center on the stage and podium area.

Your special camera is now observing the audience's "emotional focus lines" being directed and focused towards the front of the room. Perhaps they are not fully focused as conversations end, but they align with each other with ever increasing intensity as the moderator begins to welcome everyone and introduce the speaker.

Our special camera now can visually demonstrate why we get nervous speaking to a group. Like the spines of a fan, focus lines center on one subject together. The full force and intensity of the audience's emotion and feelings are on one target…the Moderator.

When that focus is on an individual, it is a very powerful and totally unique human communications relationship. This intense emotional focus may unnerve even the most experienced public speaker, and it is what scares the "*HELL*" out of you. It is an early sign that your "Tiger" is lurking nearby.

EMOTIONAL FOCUS

And now the first object lesson of how to overcome speaker's fear is available to you. Audience concentrated "emotional focus" is the primary cause of speaker's fear.

The best and most logical approach to reducing or eliminating speaker's fear is to reduce concentrated personal focus by deflecting or diffusing it. Ideas and techniques for deflecting or diffusing emotional focus of the audience from you are covered in detail in the next chapter, and throughout the remainder of this book.

However with the understanding that intense emotional focus is primary cause of speaker's fear, you can already deduce that the most common form of deflection of focus is the use of the podium. That is why you and countless others may "hide" behind the podium, and grip it tightly. It is the natural thing to do. Reducing the target you present to your audience reduces the impact. But the best that strategy yields is "White Knuckle Speaking", and you don't want to be there.

"IT IS MY PLEASURE TO INTRODUCE..."

Let's return to the meeting room and your "special camera", to observe the audience's emotional focus change from above while the speaker is being introduced.

Even before her name is spoken our speaker begins to feel nervous, partially due to her anticipation, but also because the audience is beginning to focus on her. Some in the audience are already shifting in their seats, moving to look at her prior to her introduction. Our camera records all of it.

After her name is called, our speaker rises and approaches the podium to polite applause and as the applause fades, all attention in the room is focused on her. The videotape you are recording is geometrically balanced with all lines in the room converging on one spot. The speaker!

An important point to understand, at this point, is that the focal point of emotional focus on the speaker began a few moments before she was introduced, and developed to maximum strength as she rose and walked towards the podium.

If you have experienced speaker's fear, you will know that although you think you will be all right, pangs of fear begin in your stomach in the few moments before you speak, and crescendo to outright trauma when you are introduced. It is at its highest point when you stand and face the audience.

I think the Wizard, in the "Wizard of Oz", had this problem solved very well. He spoke from behind a curtain, with his voice and image altered and amplified for audience dominating impact. With this role reversal, he was omnipotent...but when Dorothy pulled back the curtain, he faltered and was exposed.

THE INTENSITY BUILDS

In our earlier example, the focal point of the audience moved with the speaker as she transited the stage, and stabilized on the speaker as she stopped behind the podium. Concomitant with the increasing change in focus is an increasing level of emotional intensity. This is the moment of truth. Is our speaker going to handle the pressure, or will this be her "Hubert Horatio Hornblower" moment?

The central issue facing our speaker is to either absorb the intense emotional focus of the audience directly or attempt to deflect or diffuse it. All speakers experience these challenges to their confidence. It is at this moment that you as the speaker have the responsibility to seize control of the situation and harness the emotion to be used to your advantage. This is when you begin to tame your "Tiger", and you begin with a pause.

A pause at this moment is a powerful act of command. Famous statesman and legendary orator Winston Churchill, stated "Avoid speaking as long as possible, wait until your audience thinks you have nothing to say; then begin".

At the end of the pause, smile and begin to reduce the intensity of the emotional focus spotlighted on you by protecting yourself with the tools of deflection and diffusion. If you don't, you will grab the podium with a death-grip and suffer the trials and tribulations of "White Knuckle Speaking"!

PROTECTION

Intense emotional focus causes normal human reactions...self-consciousness, and fear of personal embarrassment. These feelings in turn, cause you to feel uncomfortable and be out of your comfort zone. You will naturally seek protection.

When you go to the beach, you seek protection from the sun with sunglasses, suntan oil, or protective clothing such as hats, or T-shirts. A similar situation occurs when you protect yourself from rain with an umbrella, or from the cold with a coat. These protection devices are all tools, which you select to use to solve a particular personally uncomfortable situation. There are tools you can use in public speaking that are also protection devices from the "Tiger".

The fundamental tools you need to use to overcome speaker's fear, and tame the "Tiger", are *deflecting* or *diffusing* the emotional focus upon you, so that you can do what you came there to do. *COMMUNICATE, WITHOUT FEAR!*

THREE SUMMARY THOUGHTS:

1. Understanding the impact of emotional focus between you and your audience will help you learn how to tame your "Tiger".

2. The intensity of emotional focus is the primary cause of speaker's fear, and you can begin to neutralize its effect with a pause and a smile.

3. Deflecting or diffusing focus are the two major protective tools for your use in overcoming speaker's fear.

CHAPTER 4

▼

DEFLECTION AND DIFFUSION TECHNIQUES

Diffusing or deflecting the audience's emotional focus from you are the *most powerful* tools you can apply to reduce or even eliminate speaker's fear, or "WHITE KNUCKLE SPEAKING".

LOVING THE FOCUS

In my youth, I eagerly looked forward to the annual visit of "*The Greatest Show on Earth*"...the circus. There was always a sparkle of excitement at the circus that captured me then, and I confess, still does today. There were the bright colors, music, daredevils, animal acts and clowns. However, one particular act was, and still remains, special to me; the high-wire act.

Public speaking is similar to the high-wire act, in the aspect that all eyes in the audience are riveted on the speaker; as they are on the wirewalkers, at the circus.

Do you remember being at the circus as a child? Can you recall the audience driven to attention on the high wire by the Ringmaster, as the bright spotlight illuminated sparkling sequined figures, high above the darkened arena? As the act progresses, increasingly more difficult feats are executed until finally, as emotionally stimulating music is played, the Ringmaster announces the famous "Death Defying Feat".

If you could employ the special "emotional focus" camera, used in Chapter 2 to view all of the action under the big tent, what would you see? Would it possibly be a similar image to that which you observed when our speaker stood before her audience? Correct, you would see a fan like set of lines intently focused on the high wire artist.

Also the emotions of the audience would be further intensified; orchestrated by carefully selected music and lighting to control and direct audience attention. In the circus (where they know how to tame "Tigers") intensifying the emotional focus is done purposely to maximize audience participation, build excitement, and in the long run, sell tickets.

How much would you pay for a circus ticket, if it were only to watch someone walk across the parking lot? Not much! The reason you go to the circus is to be "thrilled" by exciting acts. In essence you go because those on the wire *may* fall, but yet you are thrilled when they make it. The circus extracts or manages "emotional focus" from the audience to their advantage by first maximizing it and then capitalizing on it for their advantage. These are seasoned professionals, *"loving the focus"*.

In this book, you too are learning to manage "emotional focus" from your potential audience, however instead of maximizing it, as they do in a circus, as a "WHITE KNUCKLE SPEAKER", you are trying to *minimize* it. The circus used the tools of music and lights to intensify the focus, deflection and diffusion are the tools you will use to reduce the focus.

DEFLECTION AND DIFFUSION

As a public speaker you have an audience that, similar to the one at the circus, that has special expectations. Typically they are interested in your subject, and most importantly, they expect the speaker to be knowledgeable. These expectations are why the audience's focus is intently on the speaker.

Depending on expertise, speakers with advanced skills can capitalize on this emotional intensity with a performance that excites the audience; as did the performance of the high-wire walker. Or, if less experienced, the speaker may elect to **deflect** and **diffuse** the focused intensity of the audience with techniques that will reduce the speaker's personal feelings of nervousness and fear. These specific techniques will teach you how to tame your "Tiger", and they will also assist you to graduate from the corps of "WHITE KNUCKLE SPEAKERS".

COMMUNICATION

To this point, this book has analyzed what causes the "Tiger" to appear and cause speaker's fear. Now the spotlight shifts to the techniques of deflecting and diffusing emotional focus, the two most elemental activities you can do to begin to tame your "Tiger", and reduce speaker's fear.

COmmunication assumes two people exchanging ideas or information. A major contributor to speaker's fear is that you are not just talking conversationally with a small group of people, but you are outside of your comfort zone talking to many. The communication paradigm, that you are used to, is altered and out of balance. If you were able to diffuse or deflect some of the emotional focus the you fear the audience will bestow upon you, you could rebalance the equation and feel less self-conscious.

The overdosing of your nervous systems with adrenaline, at the beginning of a speech, takes approximately two or three minutes to process out of your body. It is during this period of time that you apply diffusion and deflection techniques to help you rebalance your emotional equation and return to some degree of normalcy. As a result of these actions you will drive your rate of fear downward and become more comfortable in resuming person-to-person *com*munications.

It has been established; that it is the intensely emotional focus of others on you, in a manner with which you are not familiar, that causes you to leave your comfort zone, becoming vulnerable and fearful. This focus causes you to walk where the "Tiger" walks, and creates nervous anxiety that translates to speaker's fear. Therefore you should explore techniques to prepare for this "moment of truth".

Learning and applying deflection and diffusion techniques is critical to successfully negotiating the two to three minutes of speaker's fear you will face at the beginning of your speech. Deflection and diffusion techniques are the main tools with which you can tame your "Tiger".

DEFLECTION TECHNIQUES

The "magic" of magic is based on illusion. Illusion, or causing your mind to see and believe something that isn't real is based on deflection techniques. When a magician asks you to look inside his hat, or to peer into a box to verify that it is empty, you should watch his other hand, because that is where he doesn't want you to watch. He is taking control of the situation by deflecting your attention to where he wants it to be, (away from him).

The same principle applies to you as a public speaker, planning to be in control and deflecting the audience's emotional focus away from you, is the best technique possible to reduce or eliminate speaker's fear.

If only you could hold up a mirror to reflect the emotion focused towards you back to the audience. But alas, no mirror like that exists. Or what if you could borrow the curtain and the amplifier from the Wizard of Oz to use as a shield behind which you could hide, and speak without fear of facing your audience. The sad news is those are whimsical options, and they won't help you solve the very real problems you face. Real tools to help you are deflection and diffusion.

Deflection is the act of shifting all of the audience's emotional focus from you to something or someone else. The deflection needs only to be significant enough to move the focal point of the emotional focus from you to overcome your anxiety at the beginning of your speech.

A FRIEND IN NEED

A close friend of mine, who is a technology executive at The Walt Disney Co., once approached me to help him prepare for a particularly challenging speech on technology he was to give to a group of nationally recognized medical technologists who specialized in prosthesis devices.

Although an experienced speaker, he was quite apprehensive at presenting to this particular group of medical experts, which included several Nobel Prize winners. He confided in me, "If I can only get started on the right foot, I know I will be able to give a meaningful, and well appreciated speech, but I don't know this audience, and to be honest, I'm nervous about this presentation".

I explained to him the advantages of using deflection and diffusion techniques and we set about discussing what topic related technique he could use to overcome his anxiety. We chose a uniquely Disney item, the animatronic hand of Abraham Lincoln from the Hall of Presidents exhibit in Disney World.

Thinking about the ability to deflect the emotional focus away from himself by holding the "hand" high in the air, and asking the audience if they knew the source, was all he needed. He never took the hand with him, but he did take a picture. He formulated the start of his speech to deflect attention to the picture with rhetorical questions about animatronics, and the impact that unique technology, such as that researched by the Walt Disney Company, might have on future development of prosthesis devices.

The reviews of his speech were excellent, he wasn't nervous when he began, and he thoroughly enjoyed speaking that evening. Why…because he never let his "Tiger" out of its cage. Once he figured out how to get through the potential rush of speaker's fear using deflection, it was smooth sailing.

Other representative deflection techniques are:

1. Place a topic related object under a cloth on a table near the podium. After your beginning pause and smile, reach slowly towards the cloth and remove it with a flourish. Pause again, and rhetorically ask the audience, "What do you think that is?

2. Before you start speaking use the "Before I start" opening. Plan to introduce someone, or identify something that will help you deflect focus away from you. For example, in a speech where you are planning to present some new or different ideas, pre-select someone (Gary Hahn in this example) to participate with you, and start your speech with something like this.
    "Before I start, I would like to ask Gary Hahn to come up and help me with something". Hold up a dollar bill. "Gary, will you exchange a dollar with me?" The audience will probably murmur and kibitz with Gary about this being a trick or something, which will only help deflect the emotional focus from you.
    After you exchange dollars, thank Gary and have him be seated, then state the following to the audience; "When we are finished exchanging dollars, we each have only one dollar again. It was an even exchange. But, if we exchange ideas, as I hope we will here today, we will all leave with more than we came with."

Either of these tools will help you tame your "Tiger".

DIFFUSION TECHNIQUES

Similar to the effect of deflection, diffusion also will reduce your speaking anxiety by redirecting the audience's emotional focus. Deflection takes the emotional focus as it is and redirects it from you to something else through substitution. Diffusion divides the emotional focus into smaller units, reducing its impact on you.

A good diffusion technique is an audience questionnaire that you direct be completed before you start. Another is the use of a visual, such as a demonstration device or a slide, poster or overhead projection. These types of activities allow you to direct attention (their emotional focus) away from you, towards the devices you select, diffusing the focus (remember the camera) from you to your selected visual.

QUESTIONNAIRE

Imagine walking into the meeting room to hear a speech on Positive Mental Attitude (P.M.A.), and you see bright green pieces of paper on every chair. You select your seat, pick up the paper, and read it. It asks you to help make this evening a success by writing down the answers to two questions about your mental attitude. You are then instructed to fold your answer sheet, and put it away until the next morning, when it will benefit you.

What do you think about as you answer the questions? Do you talk about the question with your friends or associates? Doesn't completing a questionnaire before the speech begins change the paradigm you expected? Does it alter what you are thinking about as the speaker is introduced? Odds are the questionnaire diffused your emotional focus. **THAT WAS ITS PURPOSE!!**

To make the above-discussed questionnaire even more diffusing, the speaker could have added a line at the bottom of the questionnaire, that during the speech, he would ask for three members of the audience to share their answers with the audience.

The potential that you may have to share perhaps quite personal answers will further shift your emotional focus from the speaker, to you. And it will do the same to every audience member. With this technique the speaker has removed the "Tiger" from his path and put it squarely on yours.

The purpose of learning and utilizing techniques such as these is to help you graduate from the ranks of "White Knuckle Speaking". This is done by helping you navigate through the first few minutes of fear and trauma with deflection and diffusion techniques, which eliminate the root cause of speaker's fear, emotional focus. From the example above, you can see how good planning in this area will help you achieve your goal.

Other representative diffusion techniques are:

1. Utilizing a subject related quiz, "assess" your audience's subject knowledge, before you start. Give the answers publicly and have the audience grade their own papers, or their neighbors. The individual competitive spirit of the audience will remove their focus from you and turn it inward.

2. Ask for volunteers from the audience to assist you later in your speech. If you have an activity or an example later in your remarks, this technique is very diffusing at the start. Even if you don't use the volunteers, it won't be a big problem later for most in the audience will forget.

3. Ask for a show of hands, for or against for some question relating to your subject. Make a big show out of counting the hands, and look towards the back of the audience to ask, "Are you voting or waving at me?" I assure you the audience will chuckle and be sufficiently diffused.

There are other topic related activities that may use deflection or diffusion techniques for your speeches. Use those recommended here for starters, and in time you will create your own.

THE DREADED JOKE

The customary opening joke is a diffusion technique. The audience focuses on the joke, and when it ends they laugh individually and together. That is, if they think it's funny!

Over the years it has become the custom for speakers to start with a joke, and the audience seems trained to expect one. This is a convention we all have come to expect, because it has been used as a diffusion technique for so long. Some individuals sometimes feel compelled to begin their speeches with a joke. This is a mistake!

Telling jokes, is a difficult business, and the downside risk for one that misses its mark is much greater than the potential reward. In a nutshell...**Don't Tell Jokes!!** I have rarely heard an opening joke that meets the following required three criteria for inclusion:

1. It should be funny.
2. It must not be offensive to anyone in the audience.
3. The joke's theme should be related to the subject of your speech.

Although I believe I have a pretty good sense of humor, and a true sense of timing for jokes I do not use jokes to diffuse audience focus, and I will not recommend the use of jokes to begin a speech to anyone.

DIFFUSION AND DEFLECTION SUMMARY

Diffusion and deflection approaches should be planned within a structure of effectiveness. The next two chapters of this book will focus on speech structure and effectiveness that will help you to minimize speaker's fear through diffusion and deflection while maximizing the effectiveness of your message.

Let's end this chapter where we began:

Diffusing or deflecting the audience's emotional focus from you are the *most powerful* tools there are to reduce or even eliminate speaker's fear, or **"White Knuckle Speaking"**.

THREE SUMMARY THOUGHTS:

1. Diffusing or deflecting the audience's emotional focus from you are the *most powerful* tools available to reduce or eliminate speaker's fear or "White Knuckle Speaking".

2. Learn to "Love the focus"! The exhilarating feeling of a speaker's "high" you will experience at the end of your speech, begins by managing emotional focus during the first two to three minutes of your speech.

3. Until you are more experienced, and have your "Tiger" fully trained, avoid the potentially dangerous joke.

▼

PART TWO

PREPARATION WITH STRUCTURE

BUILDING A "TIGER" CAGE

CHAPTER 5

▼

THE BASICS

DEVELOPING YOUR SPEECH

Once you have volunteered or have been selected to give a presentation, you are past the point of no return. You are on the trail to fight your "Tiger", and need to fully prepare to ensure you come back alive. Speech preparation will take longer than you think, for it includes several levels of activity that will lead to a more meaningful and professional presentation.

Activities will include steps such as assembling ideas, researching data, assembling topic related anecdotes, working to structure and sequence your material to be most effective, creatively tuning your material to engage your audience, and inserting speaker's fear reduction techniques.

It was Mark Twain who said; *"It takes me about three weeks to prepare an impromptu speech."* Many professional speechwriters use the rule of thumb that it takes about one hour of preparation for every minute of speech.

Methodologies for collecting information and assembling it in a professional manner are varied and highly personal. I use 3x5 note cards, but you may use any vehicle with which you are comfortable. There are, however some fundamentals to follow whichever method you choose.

Assuming you do use index cards, because they are portable, flexible and allow you sort and assemble your thoughts in a useful manner, start by writing a "D" in the upper left corner of two or three cards and set them aside for later use. From this point, the best process to follow for proven success is to start by deciding and stating the objective or goal of your presentation.

It cannot be emphasized enough, how important selecting a goal, at this time, is to reducing your speaking anxiety. In your journey to find and tame the "Tiger", it is critical to know exactly where you are going. Planning a speech is similar to planning a vacation trip, you need both a target destination and a map to be successful. The destination is your goal, and the map is the structure to facilitate getting there. The next chapter will focus on structure, it's now time to focus on and select your goal.

TARGET YOUR AUDIENCE

Identifying your goal by *writing it down* is the starting point. This will be the first of many index cards you complete as you develop the basics of your speech. To ensure your goal is sharply focused, you will need to complete a sentence similar to this:

As a result of my presentation I would like the audience to _____.

To help you with developing your goal, ask yourself: What it is you have been asked to accomplish in your speech or presentation? What would you like to communicate with your speech? What would you like the audience to do as a result of your speech or presentation?

My experience has led me to conclude that the best type of question to ask at this time is *action* oriented, and centered on the audience. Ask yourself what you would like them to do when your speech ends. Do you want them to vote for you? Support a new tax levy? Be entertained? Donate to a specific cause? Buy your product? The target of what you want them to do is the primary consideration for choosing the starting point of your remarks.

Another consideration for targeting your goal is the make up of the audience. Your goal presenting the same subject may vary by the audience. Are they business people, an association, a social club, children, or a political action committee? Their ability to commit group resources or make only personal decisions would obviously influence your selected presentation goal.

Come to grips with what you want them to do then write it down on the card. What you write down will be your action statement for getting your audience committed. You will learn to develop it more completely in the next chapter, which deals with structure. It is the destination or goal of your presentation. Once you have established where you are going, you can begin to fully develop your presentation.

RESEARCH...THE BEGINNING

There are four categories of structure (**I-D-E-A**) that a successful speech must follow, and this structure will be covered in detail in the next chapter. Your research, however, should **NOT** be collected or categorized into any pre-selected structure, at this time, for that would potentially limit the scope of your research. For now you should just be prolific at writing thoughts and facts down on cards to assemble the basics of your speech.

Start with a listing of ideas you have about the subject. Don't worry about listing three, ten, or twenty-five; for they will later consolidate and change as your speech develops. Talk with others about your ideas and also solicit their opinions and ideas. Write down anything that crosses your mind relating to your speech. Add anecdotes, stories, opinions or anything that may potentially be related to your subject.

After a few days of jotting down index cards, it's time to begin to sort them into a usable order. This activity is up to you to perform as best you can, because only you will have a sense of what you have assembled, its meaning and importance.

Although there is no standard methodology for this activity, I recommend the following general approaches to the task:

1. Try to choose three to five major subjects you feel you would like to communicate in your speech. If you have subjects already written on index cards, select them out. If not, write the major subjects on index cards and lay them out in front of you.

2. Sort all of your index cards into the three to five major subject piles you have selected. View these piles as chapters to a book that you will use to tell your story. Chapter 6 will introduce you to developing "Examples" for effective speaking, and these major subjects will be the foundation for developing them.

3. Prioritize the subjects into a sequence that best represents your feelings about the subject you have chosen. Place the most important first, and continue in descending order.

4. Copy your "goal card" and place it at the front and back of the pack.

5. Retrieve the cards upon which you wrote a "D" in the upper left hand corner. Review your material and design whatever topic related deflection or diffusion techniques you feel will be effective for your speech and write them down. Insert the "D" cards immediately after your first and leading goal card.

This order of development has been found to be constructive for me, for it is not rigid, and will not restrict developmental thoughts or create mental "blocks". You will want to add additional cards, as new or different thoughts occur to you during the continued development of your speech.

From this point on, your work will become more traditional. Now you should begin to read and reread your stack of cards, editing, altering and updating as you see fit. You will find that you will often change card sequence as your familiarity with your research improves, and logical groupings form in your mind.

Read through your cards frequently, and as you draw nearer to writing your speech, you will find that task will be remarkably easy. You will eventually construct your final speech considering *all* of the structural, environmental, and fear reduction techniques covered in this book. Your ability to reduce speaker's fear, and to tame your "Tiger", will be in direct correlation to your ability to include the full range of speaking techniques presented in "White Knuckle Speaking"!

CREATIVITY…THE DIFFERENCE

Once you have finished a relatively complete outline of your potential speech, you should first begin a multiple revision process with a revision of creativity. Remember, your end product will be communications between people, and the more unique or special your remarks are the more impact they will have.

Surely you can remember being put to sleep by a dry, boring speaker. The addition of a creativity revision cycle to your work, at this time, will make a very positive difference in how your speech is received.

It's time to bring both your completed work and your creativity together. The task is to develop a creative version of each of the three to five major subjects you have chosen, to improve interest and retention. A technique I use in my creativity revision is to write my revision ideas on the back of the index cards, using different color ink. I truly don't know how much the different color really helps, but it works for me.

CREATIVITY ON DEMAND

Often it is difficult to be creative on demand, which is why it is hard to remember jokes when someone says, "Tell a joke". To help you over this hurdle, the best way to foster creativity is to share your ideas or thoughts with others and ask them for their ideas. Alone doesn't do it. Friends can help!

You may want to carry major subject index cards with you throughout the day, and when you are with a friend, describe the point you want to make on the card, and your thoughts of how to do it. You will be amazed at the lubricating effect of this type of conversation to creativity. Before too long you will have multiple new creative options for your use.

It is up to you to keep your index cards updated at their latest level of development, so as I said earlier, get used to rewriting and revisions. After you have rewritten your cards, don't stop talking to others and seeking their ideas from your new revised perspective. The more discussions you have, the more changes you make…the more effective your speech.

WINNERS AND EVERYONE ELSE

On the P.G.A. tour, after 72 holes of championship golf, the average scores of the second through fifth place finishers is less than three strokes behind the winner. At this level of competition there is not much difference between winning and everything else, except perhaps one or two creative shots struck during the tournament that sets the winner apart from the field.

One P.G.A. member who is most celebrated for his creative shot making is the world renowned Spaniard, Seve Ballesteros. His creative approach to golf shots is legendary, and respected by his peers. There are few trouble situations on a golf course that can beat Seve's skills. To understand why he has a unique approach to shot making, you must only understand that he grew up learning an playing the game of golf with only a single club; a five iron.

Utilizing this single club for long and short distances, low and high trajectory, sand, as well as draw and fade shots trained him to mentally approach every shot he faces with many more options than his competitors.

Your mental approach to public speaking, like that of Seve Ballesteros' approach to golf, should be fresh and full of creative thoughts. Eventually, as a result, you will not only prepare better, but you will find yourself a winner and not just one of the rest.

In speaking, as in golf, you need good fundamentals and practice to be successful. But to help you tame the "Tiger" of speaker's fear, you need to mix in creativity. With creativity, you will control more of the speaking process, your subject will be better received and with the confidence you will gain from knowing you have well prepared, interesting material. As a result your confidence will improve and your personal anxiety will lessen.

EVEN ECONOMICS CAN BE FUN!

Creativity can be applied to every subject. To prove that point, the subject of economics has been selected to demonstrate how creativity can liven up a planned presentation on this potentially dreary subject.

Consider, for example, these two creative ways to present economic information on a four trillion dollar trade deficit. An audience may have a difficult time grasping the size or scope of a trillion dollars. Try explaining it in these creative terms and see if it won't be measurably more meaningful:

1. If you stacked $1000 bills in your hand to a height of four inches you would be holding one million dollars. For you to hold one trillion dollars, that four-inch pile of one thousand dollar bills would have to become 76 miles high.
2. To understand the significance of one trillion dollars, consider that if you set aside one million dollars a day, every day, from the year 1 AD until today, you would not yet have a trillion dollars.
3. To reach one trillion dollars, you would have to continue setting aside one million dollars a day for the next 7 1/2 centuries or until approximately 2750 AD.

The point here is that with a little bit of creativity, a story can be told with impact. If it can be done with economics, it can be done with any subject.

DRAMA

As the circuit preacher ascended the courthouse stairs to begin his Sunday sermon to the gathered townspeople on a crisp fall morning in 1883, a hush rolled over the crowd. Commanding their attention with a dramatic pause, the preacher slowly reached into his pocket, pulled out a handkerchief and wiped his brow.

Then he uttered his first words, *"God Damn it's HOT out here today!"* The townspeople recoiled from the preacher's vulgarity and began to talk to each other, at first in a murmur, but then as a rising crescendo of noise until the preacher yelled. *"That's what I heard a man in this very crowd say this beautiful Sunday morning; and I was offended by his remarks...therefore I will preach today on "The Sins of Blasphemy!"*

The affect of mixing creativity with drama when speaking to an audience did not escape this 19th century orator. Why let it escape you?

THREE SUMMARY THOUGHTS:

1. Start with the ending to help you establish your speaking goals. Target your audience, so that your goals match their capability to respond.

2. Utilize the flexibility of index cards, or the medium of your choice, as an aid to help you capture and formulate a sound speech outline.

3. Use creativity to develop interesting speaking material, and another person as a "sounding board" for ideas to improve your creative juices.

Chapter 6

—————————— ▼ ——————————

Structuring Your Presentation

"IDEA" THE KEYWORD TO SUCCESS

Let's briefly look at the four fundamental components of **I-D-E-A** in a short preview before you explore each segment in detail:

INTRODUCTION—Get this one right, because its effectiveness will set the tone for the rest of your presentation. Design the "**I**" component of **IDEA** to be one or two sentences in length. The purpose of the Introduction is to rivet the audience to both you and your subject. It is only a teaser designed to command attention from your audience to prepare them for your remarks.

DRAWING IN—Also brief in length, the "**D**" component of **IDEA** is designed to convince the audience of the reason or merit of listening to the remainder of your presentation.

EXAMPLES—Much of the Bible is written in parables to ensure the story message is clearly understood. Analogies and parables are examples that graphically communicate the desired manner in the most effective manner. The "E" component of **IDEA** is the heart of your presentation, the pros and cons of which are best illustrated to your audience's minds through the use of Examples.

ACTION—Action means *ACTION!!* The closing section of any effective presentation seeks commitment to action. The "A" component, like the "I" component, should be one or two sentences in length.

I-D-E-A, a wonderful tool for you to use every time you wish to develop a presentation. Let's explore this innovative tool for presentation structure in greater depth. Assume you have written your **ACTION** goal for this presentation, you now are ready to better understand and develop your Introductory statements.

I=INTRODUCTION

"I was careening from an exploded front tire, when the fingers of the guardrail grasped the front of my car and with metal groaning, hurled us into quiet flight.

Plummeting towards the rocks below, I chose not to jump free, but to lie over my daughter sparing her from certain death. Why had I not driven more cautiously I asked myself as the sharp impact stole my consciousness".

This is an example of an excellent Introductory sentence for a speech on safe driving. The Introduction to your speech must be captivating to your audience. The most effective Introductory statement is composed of one to three sentences which command the audience's attention through the spoken word. The goal is to emotionally slap the audience to attention with a verbal 2 X 4. The objective of the "I" component of your speech is to demand attention with words of strong personal impact.

The Introductory statement may be an imaginary situation, as given above, or a challenging question, or declarative sentence, such as:

Challenging Question—
Why do you care enough to buy life insurance, to protect your family, and yet drive without wearing your seatbelts?

Declarative Sentence-
Considering National Safety Council statistics, one of you in the audience here tonight will be killed in a car accident this weekend.

You can almost feel the power of these Introductory sentences, as you read them. Compare them to a typical sentence used to introduce a safe driving speech…"As another Holiday weekend approaches, I want to once again remind you to drive carefully."

The purpose of the Introductory sentence in **IDEA** is to rivet the audience's attention to both you and the topic. **PLAN IT THAT WAY!!**

D=DRAWING IN

Let's revisit, for a moment, the "I" statement about safe driving provided above:

"I was careening from an exploded front tire, when the fingers of the guardrail grasped the front of my car and with metal groaning, hurled us into quiet flight.

Plummeting towards the rocks below, I chose not to jump free, but to lie over my daughter sparing her from certain death. Why had I not driven more cautiously I asked myself as the sharp impact stole my consciousness".

And now, we draw them in with a strong "D" statement:

"What a traumatic moment, that could have been avoided, with proper planning. If you will just listen to me for the next few minutes, I will share with you three safe driving tips that will prevent a tragic situation like this from ever occurring to you. If you listen carefully, what I will share with you could even extend your life as much as 20 years."

Can you see how the previous three "D" sentences **Draw** *you* in? They are designed to make *you* want to listen. They explain *WHY* you want to listen to the message that follows. What the "D" sentences accomplish is the same thing a fire insurance salesman accomplishes by showing you pictures of a crying family huddled outside their burning house, "as interest".

By now you may be asking yourself, how do you know the audience's interest? The answer is you may not! However, you are designing your presentation to achieve a specific action oriented goal, so you must plan both your "I" and "D" statements to create a reason to listen.

One tip to make your "Drawing In" sentences as effective as they can be, is to include the word "you" in them, which links your audience to the subject by creating personal interest.

"Drawing In" the audience establishes communications control, and it serves as a bridge into the body of your presentation. The **D**rawing in sentences also are additive with the Introduction sentences to jointly form a relatively significant period of time which helps you through the most nerve-wracking segment of your speech. The structural function if **I-D-E-A** is also a superior tool for reducing speaking anxiety and attaining the skill to tame the "Tiger".

E=EXAMPLES

The age old axiom; "*Tell 'em what your gonna tell 'em, tell 'em, and then tell 'em what you told 'em*"…applies here. Another traditional speaker's axiom that "*The mind will only hold what the seat of the pants will endure*" also applies.

The majority of what you say in front of a group will be not heard, not understood or forgotten. Therefore when preparing the main portion or body of your presentation from your note cards, you must prepare to speak in a manner which ensures a maximum level of understanding and retention in your audience. The best way to do that is with Examples.

The Bible is full of anecdotes, analogies, parables and examples, all designed to ensure clarity of understanding, throughout the ages and across many lands. Examples, because of their mental vividness, allow you to communicate to your audience on a common plane of understanding, and they heighten both understanding and retention.

There are three steps to structuring effective Examples in your speech.

STEP 1. Write down the objective of your presentation.

STEP 2. Write down two or three reasons why you think the objective written in Step 1 is important.

STEP 3. Develop two or three EXAMPLES for each of the reasons listed in Step 2. The examples must be at a common (high) level of communication to ensure group understanding of, and commitment to your message.

Let me give you an example, *(Notice what I am doing!)*, of what I mean:

STEP 1—*OBJECTIVE*—To ensure the audience is so aware of the dangers associated with driving, that they use their seatbelts, to reduce personal injury, in case of an accident.

STEP 2—*REASON*—Accidental injuries and deaths in motor vehicles, can be reduced with consistent use of automobile safety devices, such as seatbelts.

STEP 3—*EXAMPLE*—(**An analogy**) Picture yourself, seated on a bench, in the fast lane of an interstate highway, with cars and trucks zipping by at speeds in excess of 65 miles per hour. Are you nervous? Would you like to move to safety?

Let's up the ante on this situation, by moving the bench along the highway, at 70 M.P.H. You are slipping and sliding on the bench as it swerves in and out of traffic. How do you feel now? Are you holding on tightly? Would you wear a seatbelt, if one were available?

(A speaker can develop these examples even more graphically, by adding other dangerous circumstances, such as: wrapping metal around you, tying a 25 gallon container of gasoline to the rear of the bench, and adding a red hot engine with pistons churning, belts turning and gears whining, between your legs. At what point of increasing danger would you commit to wearing a seatbelt as a safety device? What reason do you have to not wear your seatbelt today on the way home, and every time you drive from now on.)

Example–(An anecdote)

We'll call him Jack. Jack and I grew up together in Cincinnati, Ohio, laughing together as we learned of life, and dreaming the idealistic dreams of young men in the glory of the Fifties. Ours was a limitless future, there for the taking, if only we worked and prepared for it and its splendor. It's ironic that only one of us has pursued those shared dreams, while the other never left the fifties.

It was a horrifying car crash that fate used as a selection instrument to determine which of us would live and which would remain enshrined in the fifties. Many times I replay the tragic event in my mind, a straight dry road, not going particularly fast, and then the speeding truck veering towards us. Jack swerved to avoid a head-on collision, and we struck that large tree with stunning impact.

I was wedged in the car for over an hour as rescuers fought to extricate me. I was held captive there, during the crash by my seatbelt, and after it by twisted metal and shards of glass. Jack was thrown clear of it all, and he landed in a flowerbed of pansies, where he died.

To this day, whenever in a car, I remember to use seatbelts and expect all others with me to do the same. When I see pansies, I always think of my friend Jack, robbed of his future by his failure to wear his seatbelt.

If you care for your future, or that of those you love, when you ride in a car, wear seat belts, and whenever you see pansies, think of Jack.

The examples just given were directed to the audience at a "high plane" of communications. They would be successfully understood because everyone in the audience would be empathetic with the situations, and relate to the descriptions.

Examples that utilize technical jargon, "inside" stories or jokes should be avoided. You must ensure that the Examples you select, are oriented to the same communications plane on which your audience is operating. Once you select the appropriate Examples, remember to use the creative construction techniques covered in Chapter 5, to optimize the effectiveness of your message.

EXAMPLE STRUCTURE SUMMARY

The main portion (The "E" section) of your presentation should be structured with the following format:

After you have grabbed them with your "I" and reeled them in with your "D", the first paragraph of your "E" should address your objective. *(Tell 'em what you're gonna tell 'em!)* The second will begin the series of three Examples you have chosen. *(Tell em!)* And then when the three Examples have made your points, end the "E" section with a final Example designed to be a restatement of your objective. *(Tell 'em what you told 'em!)*

Sophocles said: "*To speak much is one thing, to speak well another.*" Three to five good, creative Examples are plenty to make your point for each of your major subjects or ideas. Don't confuse length with effectiveness.

A=ACTION

Now you end the structural preparation of your speech, where you began, with a commitment to **ACTION!** The goal of your speech you wrote on the first index card, is now to be attained.

This portion of your speech is required to gain commitment to a specific action you seek from the audience. As the "**I**" and "**D**" sections of your speech were brief, the "**A**" section should also be brief, perhaps only one or two sentences long. There are two reasons for brevity in your Action statement:

1. The Action statement of your speech is what the audience will go home with. Like a boxer's jab, it should be direct and sharply aimed right at your target to have the most impact.

2. Typically, "White Knuckle Speakers" are so concerned with their fears of speaking at the beginning of their speech, that they fail to recognize the euphoric feeling speakers experience at the end of their speech. This euphoria, at the conclusion, is called a speaker's "high", and it can be as strong an emotional impact as speaker's fear, only this is not the loathsome nervous feeling and topophobia, it is instead a wonderful rush of joy.

Brevity in your Action statement will allow you to memorize it, as you did your "I" and "D" statements. This memorization will assist you greatly, when you are caught up in your speaker's "high". Why risk all of your preparation and success at the end of your speech, when you are within seconds of completion.

You must include, in your Action statement, what you want your audience to do. In the case of our subject of safe driving, you want them to "Buckle up" their seat belts on the way home, throughout the long holiday weekend, and forever more.

An example of an effective action statement relating to safe driving is:

"When you leave here and put your key in the ignition tonight and every time from now on, before you turn the key…I want you to promise yourself and your loved ones that you will return safely to them, because you will wear your seatbelt and drive carefully. Do I have your commitment?"

I would now like to commit you to a bit of "**ACTION**" before you move on. Your success as a speaker will be as a result of several key activities, which are covered in this book, however one of them is **I-D-E-A** presentation structure, and you will be successful if you use it. *Will you remember, that IDEA is the keyword to success, and use it?*

STRUCTURE, BY CICERO

Structure is what makes presentations effective, and it enables the audience to carry away clear understanding of the presenter's message. Consider perhaps the most revered speaker in the last twenty centuries…Cicero. In a book titled: "On the Theory of Public Speaking", Cicero wrote six rules of discourse:

CICERO'S SIX RULES

1. INTRODUCTION—**Get attention.**
2. STATEMENT OF FACTS—**Background.**
3. DIVISION—**Items of agreement, disagreement.**
4. PROOF—**Examples of fact and evidence.**
5. REFUTATION—**Destroying adversaries' arguments.**
6. CONCLUSION—**The end.**

To think that you have been looking for an approach to speaking that would be both comfortable and effective, and all along it has been available for over twenty centuries…"**IDEA**", although contemporary, would surely be embraced by Cicero!

THREE SUMMARY THOUGHTS:

1. Preplanning an memorizing your "I", "D" and "A" statements, will carry you through the anxiety zones, and help you end with effectiveness.

2. People best understand your message when you share stories and analogies as "Examples".

3. I-D-E-A is the keyword to success.

CHAPTER 7

▼

"TIGER" TAMING PRESENTATION TOOLS

You will recall the benefits of deflection and diffusion techniques, which were covered in depth in Chapter 3. Presentation tools can divert focus from you in a similar manner, and therefore directly reduce your anxiety. They should be considered as options when you are looking for effective "Tiger" taming tools.

There are several major types of presentation tools, which are classified as audio/visual aids, or in the vernacular, A/V. They each have advantages and disadvantages for deflecting emotional focus that you should consider, as you learn and utilize these additional techniques for reducing speaker's fear.

VISUAL AIDS

Visual aids as a family of presentation tools should be considered as very positive tools to use in your quest to eliminate speaker's fear. Visual aids can be props, such as Abe Lincoln's hand, magic, a special article of clothing, a bag full of money, or any other device you dream up that will help you draw attention away from you, but still support your message.

My experience has led me to getting the "real thing", if possible, to use during my speech by passing it around to members of the audience. For example, if one of your examples refers to baseball, then get five or six baseballs and throw them out to your audience at the appropriate time in your speech. If you only have one baseball, award it to the person who asks the best question, or have the moderator award it as a door prize, at the end of your speech.

Sometimes visual aids that relate to your subject can be placed on tables and highlighted by spotlights as you speak. Other considerations for effectively using visual aids include; make cutaway models to show hidden inner workings, pre-select audience members to stand and hold a particular visual aid high for the rest of the audience to see, or to consider showcasing them in the hallway outside the meeting room, prior to your speech, or even at the conclusion of your remarks.

Used at the beginning of your speech, a visual aid will function as an excellent diffusion or deflection technique. As with any selection of an emotional focus reduction technique, your selection of a visual aid should be complementary to your total presentation.

AUDIO/VISUAL AIDS

Adding technology to visual aids allows you to provide both audio and visual stimulation to your audience. The more audience senses to which you can communicate, the more impact your presentation will have. Adding professionally designed visuals, color, motion, and sound to your speech will have the same impact that "talkies" had to silent films.

An important premise to be made at this time is best made with an analogy to the law of physics, that every action will have an equal and opposite reaction. Your use of any deflection or diffusion technique, but especially A/V, will in fact help you tame your "Tiger", and reduce speaker's fear. As an extreme example, you could elect to show a movie pertaining to your subject, and not speak at all. Or you might elect to sit out of sight behind the podium and read your speech to the audience. In both of these cases you may win the battle of speaker's fear, but you will lose the war of effective speaking.

Too much hiding will cause an equal and opposite impact on effectiveness. Therefore you must strike a balance in your choice of emotional focus reduction activities and their potential negative impact on your speech.

Compromise in this case is a necessary evil, but the balance point you will reach must consider your quest to eliminate "White Knuckle Speaking". As a novice you may choose to hide behind the podium, darken the room for a movie, or provide multiple audience quizzes. In time, as your experience builds, your balance point will move away from the extreme and towards the area of speaking effectiveness.

How you blend the anxiety reducing techniques presented in this book is entirely up to you.

A/V OPTIONS

Given your focus on reducing the anxiety of "White Knuckle Speaking", I will prioritize the major A/V options you have beginning with those which best *reduce* speaker's fear and anxiety.

FILM (16MM)

A 16mm movie has got to be at the top of any list, when reducing speaker's fear is the issue, because it is a powerful diversion technique. Professionally filmed movies are colorful, contain motion, and importantly to us, to show it you must turn the lights out.

Darkening the room to run the movie will help cover beginning anxiety through your first two to three minutes of nervousness, however, there are also some negatives to using this media. The message in the movie must match your subject, or the quality of your overall presentation will be jeopardized. Also be careful of the movie's length in relation to the time allocated for your remarks and the effect a lengthy film may take.

VCR PLAYERS

Similar to film, the basic positives and negatives attributed to movies, apply to using a VCR. One key difference to consider is that the visual impact of one or more TV screens is far less than that of the big screen movie. VCR tapes on a myriad of subjects are in abundance and it may be easier to "match" your presentation with a VCR tape than with a movie.

With a large audience, if you elect to use a VCR, ensure you schedule multiple TVs, to improve visibility. They can be easily wired together to work simultaneously from one video player, however one word of caution. Test the VCR/TV network you set up for the correct level of sound during the showing, because each TV will need to be adjusted separately, to avoid extremes of sound. Also starting and stopping the VCR tape should be practiced to avoid loud audio signal noises from TVs with blank screens.

SLIDES (35MM)

Slides will present as powerful a message as the video combined with your voice as audio. With most of the impact of a movie, as well as it's advantages and disadvantages, slides are excellent A/V options, however, they too have some unique pluses and minuses to consider.

Cost of manufacture is one of the major minuses. It is also important to obtain the right "look" or style of the slides, to ensure you leave the most professional impression possible. Consideration of items such as color, type style, as well as format and correct spelling are unusually important in this medium. All of these considerations put upward pressure on the cost of slides.

On the other hand, professionally made slides are very good A/V tools to use, because they are unique to your speech, and very catchy to the eye. Due to size constraints, they are typically in summary form and therefore help you get your message across. Obviously this summary format is highly compatible with the **I-D-E-A** structure format.

Slides are very portable, easy to carry around, and are relatively durable, especially if they are glass encased. Another plus to slides is that they act as an outline to your remarks, and can prompt you through your speech in a planned order. The downside of that advantage, however, is that to often speakers using slides, read their planned remarks, and as a result break eye contact and find it difficult to build a strong relationship with their audience.

How often have you seen the speaker get out of phase with his or her slide presentation and have to back up slides, or skip through several to get back in synch? Remember, "equal and opposite reaction".

OVERHEAD PROJECTOR

Perhaps the best and most widely used of all of the presentation tools is the overhead projector. The overhead projector again is the video component, that matched with your voice, as audio becomes a very effective tool. It has the benefit of deflecting audience emotional focus to the screen as you present your transparencies, facing the audience. Overhead projectors are the overwhelming choice of business presentations, because of their flexibility, ease of use and communications impact.

Transparencies, also known as foils or cels, are relatively inexpensive to make, easy to manufacture and are easy to correct. They are easily transportable, generated by you, so they will certainly match your speech structure, and can even be created or modified while you speak with the use of colored foil markers.

One major benefit of this versatile tool is that you face the audience during your presentation, which leads to a more effective presentation through improved "connection" with the audience.

Also a very important advantage for the "White Knuckle Speaker" exists with the use of cardboard frames for your foils. The utilization of cardboard frames for your transparencies allows you to make copious notes, reminders, and even personal reminders to yourself such as "SMILE DUMMY", around the borders.

The cardboard frames of the foils can be your friend and aide by hosting personal notes on items such as points to stress, coffee break time, humorous remarks, etc. The audience will never know of all of these crib notes, for to them you are looking at the foils as they are doing the same.

Overhead projectors are available virtually everywhere meetings are held, and can be reserved easily. If you require A/V support for your speech, you should consider this media as your first choice.

Three potential problem areas to watch out for, when using an overhead projector, are:

1. Keystoning—When the angle of the projector to the screen causes the top of the projection to loom much larger than the bottom. Not only does this look unprofessional, it makes reading your information difficult for the audience.

2. Focus—Obviously, when you test the overhead projector prior to speaking, you should focus it using one of your transparencies as a test. Not so obvious to many speakers is that while speaking the cooling fan in the projector often vibrates it out of focus during your speech. Check focus frequently!

3. Blocking—During presentations using an overhead projector, many speakers have a tendency to block the projection or line of sight to the screen with their bodies. This is because they "get into" their presentation, establish contact with their audience, and because they are facing their audience, forget to manage their presence relative to the screen behind them.

FLIPCHART

A flipchart, felt tip markers and you are good A/V tools for certain types of presentations, and they have several positive attributes. They are inexpensive, portable, obviously flexible, and allow you to create and write as you go.

A consideration about using this flexible media is that you must be careful about clarity of your penmanship and spelling errors. Mistakes in either of these two areas may reflect negatively upon your impact as a speaker.

Two tips to improve your flip chart etiquette are first, to use fresh magic markers with ample ink to ensure dark writing. Blue, black and green are the best colors. Secondly, verify that the flip chart paper has not been previously used. (Imagine turning to a "new" sheet and being embarrassed by a surprise drawing or words).

With flipcharts the lights are on and you are exposed, so there is less impact on diffusing emotional focus than several other A/V options. On the plus side, however, there is flexibility to emphasize points by writing them down as the need arises, and if prewritten, flipcharts can help you benefit from many of the advantages listed under the prior section of overhead projectors.

CHALKBOARD

There is very little advantage to using a chalkboard in reducing the anxiety of emotional focus. As an A/V tool, it has the same basic qualities as using flipcharts, however it has even more negative exposures. A chalkboard does not have color, it is more difficult to prepare, and it is easily cluttered. Other negatives include the chalkboard typically having poor contrast and the chalk dust may track to your clothes or body.

If you have no alternative, a chalkboard may be a better choice than nothing, however, given the disadvantages of it outweigh the advantages, it should be avoided if at all possible.

THE PERSONAL COMPUTER

At the base of most of the new A/V technologies is the personal computer (PC). Graphical software is now available for presentations that enhance the speaker's authority with clear, colorful presentations.

It seems like every day, that there are new programs written to assist you in developing truly effective presentations. As time goes by, this trend will certainly improve your options and effectiveness as a public speaker. PC based presentations are clearly the public speaker's technology of the future.

COMPUTER PROJECTORS

There are also new technology visual aids that are very powerful in their impact, and as with all emerging technologies they will play an ever-increasing role as A/V options.

Computer presentation projectors are relatively expensive, but highly effective. Rapidly replacing almost all other A/V devices, the projectors allow direct presentation of PowerPoint presentations from computers with motion and sound.

For the less experienced speaker trying to tame his or her "Tiger", I recommend staying away from potential technology pitfalls and complexities until ready. The "White Knuckle Speaker" should stick with the more traditional A/V support tools, over which you will have better control and confidence.

THE PODIUM

I tricked you! There is one more "Tiger" taming tool, and I have saved the best for last!

The least complex, most effective A/V tool for reducing speaker's fear, and taming the "Tiger" is the podium. Whatever you call it, the podium, rostrum, lectern, or speakers stand is an excellent presentation tool, because it is something to hide behind and grip like hell. After all if it were not for podiums to grasp there would be no "White Knuckle" speaking.

Given its practical importance, here are some tips to help you optimize your use of the podium:

1. Use it as a shield in direct proportion to your nervousness. A podium is typically big enough to hide most of your body and limit the affect of the emotional focus! USE IT! Stay behind it to "deflect" attention from the audience until you are ready to emerge.

2. When you are ready to move from behind the podium, know that moving to the side enables audience participation, and establishes a more relaxed atmosphere. If you feel you need it, remain connected to the podium with your hand or elbow, however once you move from behind it is better to stand 2-3 feet away to shift the focus to you and your subject.

3. You will probably use the podium to hold your notes, it may also be a good place to rest your hands, but be careful of making noise with them (especially if there is a microphone connected to the podium). Before you speak, check out the podium and remove anything from it that may cause noise if knocked by your hands, or even with your knees or legs.

4. Always have a glass of water (preferably with ice and lemon) under the podium. Keep it under the podium and not in sight, but place it on a cloth, or your handkerchief if you must, to prevent it from moving and spilling.

5. Formal presentation segments and your ACTION summary can be made effectively from behind the podium. Use it as a tool, not only to hide from the "Tiger", but also for the betterment of your presentation.

As a counterpoint to hiding behind a podium, I adversely select the podium to add strength to my presentation. By that I mean that I choose whenever possible to have a podium, but then I specifically avoid using it.

This technique not only directs the audience's emotional focus directly to me, but also demonstrates a differentiation of me from other more traditional speakers. When there is a podium, people expect you to use it. Not using it is dramatically more powerful and more effective if you are skilled enough to pull it off.

EFFECTIVENESS TRADE OFF

As you strive to overcome speaker's fear you will work diligently at diffusion or deflection techniques, however equal effort must be given the structure and content of the speech itself, to ensure the effectiveness of your speech is not jeopardized. All of your endeavors to tame your "Tiger", should not negatively affect the impact and effectiveness of your speech.

The effectiveness trade off, you must always make, is that by choosing a particular visual aid to maximize reduction of your speaker's fear, you will be using a deflection technique that reduces your direct involvement with your audience.

This is by no means wrong, during the minimum time (2-3 minutes) you need to "pass through" that beginning zone of anxiety you are trying to combat. The impact of this effectiveness trade off is more significantly felt throughout the remainder of your speech, because the room lighting will be reduced, and audience focus will continue to be split between you and the A/V.

Visual aids will help you. However, work hard to ensure the visual aid is used primarily as a constructive tool for anxiety reduction and that it remains helpful to your message. Most importantly, ensure your choice of a visual aid does not become only a mask to hide behind for the whole speech, as done by the ancient Greeks.

Experience teaches that if a visual aid will help you tame the "Tiger" at the beginning of your speech, by all means use one there! But, if it is at all possible, and the subject matter does not require them, refrain from using visual aids for the rest of your speech. You are much more powerful, and therefore more effective when you connect with your audience as a person, and not just be a "talking head" hiding behind the podium.

Keep in mind, however, that from the perspective of a "White Knuckle Speaker", a visual aid is a tool that you may choose to use to overcome speaker's fear. If you need the crutch of an A/V use it longer, but if you have prepared your remarks using the **I-D-E-A** structure explained in the prior chapter, you won't need as much of a crutch throughout your speech, only at the beginning. The issue is how to *best* use an A/V to do just enough fear reduction through deflection or diffusion of emotional focus, and not one scintilla more.

Here are some ideas to consider:

1. Orient the use of an A/V tool to *precede* you. If selecting a movie or a similar A/V, such as a video, plan it to play after your introduction, but before your speech. This sequencing will allow you lot's of time to "settle down" as the audience's emotional focus is diverted to the film.

    You can shake yourself silly while the room is dark and the audience is focused on the screen. You, as the speaker, will benefit from the message in the film, and so you should be reviewing your "I" and "D" statements to capture the emotion of your audience, and have your total presentation (A/V included) appear seamless to the audience.

2. Ensure you begin your remarks as soon as possible at the end of the film. Have an assistant or someone else that you have "trained", turn off the projector immediately as the film ends. Do not let the credits roll on and on. Do not wait for a "THE END" to appear, just appear at the podium "instantly" and deliver those well planned "I" and "D" statements.

3. Use a *"HOT"* screen while the audience gathers in the room. If possible, have the room lights slightly dimmed, and a slide or overhead projection showing on the screen. It is best to have the projection a logo or graphic symbol, with your name on it. This diversion technique gives you a running start at your introduction and an early linkage with your audience.

4. Write a question relating to your speech on a flipchart or chalkboard before your audience assembles. For example, if you are speaking on economics, you could write; "What are the three major segments of M1?" Have the question displayed prominently in the front of the room.

    Then, as you meet people prior to the commencement, suggest, lightly, that there will be a graded quiz of 100 economic questions later in your speech, or with a different tack you could suggest that the first person with the correct answer, will get to take your place on the podium, or win the national debt.

However you do it, the effect will be one of the best diffusion techniques you could plan for. People will focus on the question, their potential answer, the answers of others, what the real "prize" is, they will talk to each other about M1, and focus on multiple items and even have a little focus left for you. Mission accomplished!

LEVERAGE

Remember, A/V tools can be used as leverage, to help you tame the "Tiger", and reduce your level of anxiety and speaker's fear. The more anxiety you believe you will have, the more you should consider using one or more A/V tools to diffuse and deflect the emotional focus of the audience.

The more experienced you become the less dependency, or need, you will have for external assistance from A/V tools. However, no matter how good a speaker you become, you will always benefit from the wise use of both visual aids and audio/visual aids, for they will help you to be more effective. Your audience will remember more of what you say if you add visual impact to your speech planning.

THREE SUMMARY THOUGHTS:

1.   Presentation tools deflect and diffuse emotional focus from you and directly reduce your anxiety. Learn to recognize and choose the unique characteristics of each type of A/V support in the appropriate speaking situations.

2.   The boon to "White Knuckle Speakers" is the podium. Know how to use it to tame the "Tiger"!

3.   Use just enough A/V, as an emotional focus reduction technique to accomplish your objective of reducing speaker's fear.

▼

PART THREE

MORE FEAR REDUCTION TECHNIQUES

MAKING THE "TIGER" DANCE

▼

CHAPTER 8

THE ROOM

PREPARATION

The watchword for this chapter is *preparation*! Most of the physical preparation for your speech will be centered in the room in which you speak. Meeting room preparation is as fundamental to a successful speech as a foundation is to a house.

ENVIRONMENTAL IMPACT

Consideration of environmental impact issues does not just apply to endangered species such as the California condor or the spotted owl. It also applies to you in your quest to capture and tame your personal "Tiger".

Environmental impact is a surprisingly critical topic to understand, and control as you plan to reduce your anxiety when speaking to a group. What is most interesting about this subject is that, although it is one over which you may have virtually 100% control, speakers rarely capitalize on the full range of advantages they could glean from effectively managing the environmental impact of the meeting room.

You may not have control over the selection of the presentation room; however if you do, or if you can at least influence it, try to minimize the potential negative impact of noise from adjacent rooms, especially if you are speaking in a hotel environment. Many a good speech has suffered from the sound of a tray of dishes crashing to the floor, or a loud movie or music played in an adjacent meeting room.

Room scheduling considerations, to reduce the possibility of external noise impact, include:

- Corner rooms, or rooms at the end of a hallway, are preferred to reduce noise from adjacent rooms.

- If possible choose a room that has at least one vacant room separating it from the next one in use.

- Be detailed enough to check hotel setup plans for any adjacent rooms, even if they are scheduled as empty. Often, a later meeting or dinner is setup in advance, and it may be done while you are in mid-speech.

Noted public speaker Joel Weldon is known for his penchant to arrive at his speaking location a full four hours before his speaking engagement. His consistently superior performance begins with detailed professional preparation. The adage to *"Expect what you inspect"* communicates the added value of previewing the meeting room in advance of your speech.

Your responsibility to arrive early rests solely with you and your schedule planning. There are no excuses good enough to explain why you arrived late. Consider the extremes of what tragedy could potentially happen in your travels to the speaking site, and plan accordingly. If you are flying in, consider traveling one day early to avoid potential cancellations or major weather delays. If traveling, plan to stay in or near the location of your speech, and if you are a local, drive in early to ensure you have enough time to comfortably review and make necessary room changes.

To take full advantage of the positive opportunities presented by effective room management, there are three cardinal rules that must be followed. They are:

Rule 1: **GO TO THE ROOM EARLY!**
Rule 2: **GO TO THE ROOM EARLY!**
Rule 3: **GO TO THE ROOM EARLY!**

PREVIEW THE ROOM

When you first arrive, find out who is in control of the facility in which you will speak. Typically, the people with the most control of room arrangements are the hotel or building facility maintenance personnel, and you will benefit by previewing the room with them. These people can be critical to your success, so get them on your team by talking over both the direct and indirect room arrangements. Your discussion will include such basic items as heat and light settings, podium location, chair arrangements, etc.

Other very important subjects for discussion are emergency exits and emergency notification procedures. While speaking, you will be the room leader and if any emergency arose it would be your responsibility to correctly direct room evacuation.

You should review and take control of every aspect of room arrangements, no matter how trivial they may seem. Your purpose is to ensure the environment for your presentation is constructive to your efforts, and that your speech is not negatively affected by it. Your attention to detail at this moment will only help improve your effectiveness and reduce factors that could be wrong or go wrong, causing you additional stress, or anxiety.

Obviously reducing anxiety is "goodness" to someone trying to avoid, **"White Knuckle Speaking"**.

ROOM ASSESSMENT CHECKLIST

Take with you and review the checklist of considerations you should make when assessing and preparing room arrangements. The need to check the room the day before if possible, but at least prior to your presentation, cannot be over-emphasized. I have developed a checklist of room considerations and arrangements I include in my speaking acceptance package to my clients. I also give a copy of it to the facilities people, when I meet with them prior to my speech.

Here is my checklist, of room related items, that should be reviewed prior to your speaking engagement:

Assistance—Prepare, and keep with you a list of names and phone numbers of people you may want to reach before the meeting. At a minimum you should include the meeting coordinator, the meeting site address and phone number, and the same information for the sponsoring management.

Signage—As you arrive, wander around the speaking site as if you are an attendee at your speech. Is the meeting location listed at the building entrance? Is the meeting room clearly marked? If at a hotel or public building, are there directional signs that could be placed along the routes attendees will walk?

Anything you can do to make arrival for the attendees smooth and confusion free is constructive to their attitude, and therefore beneficial to you.

Refreshments—Although you will probably not be personally responsible for ordering any refreshments, you will want to ensure they are located outside the meeting room, if at all possible. The primary reason for this is noise reduction, but there are secondary benefits of increased formality and meeting punctuality from which you will benefit.

Audience supplies—Any handouts, meeting badges, pads, pencils, etc. will, like refreshments be better disbursed outside the meeting room. The lone exception to this would be any quizzes or other materials you have planned to be on the audience's seats as a focus diffusion technique.

Audience seating—The selection criteria for the form of audience seating that best helps you reduce speaker's fear and your anxiety is covered in detail later in this chapter in a section entitled "Room Layout". The reason it is on the checklist is for you to verify that the seating pattern is indeed what you requested.

Muzak/Sound systems—The first of two potential noise interruptions that need to be managed correctly are any external sound systems. These include those you see and those you don't. There may be a sound system control in the meeting room, and if so you want to turn it off, and tape it off with masking tape. *Also*, make sure you ask the facility people where the master control is, and how to ensure facility paging is turned off in your room.

Telephone—As in the case of the sound systems, covered in the preceding paragraph, telephones can also be a nuisance. Seek any telephones out in the meeting room. Don't forget to look for them behind the stage area, and in any adjacent rooms. When you find them, have them removed, and then for good measure, tape over the wall receptacles.

Room thermostat—Find the room thermostat and set it in the 65F range. The room will rapidly heat up as the audience enters, and I assure you, the room air conditioner will never catch up to the temperature you set. Any temperature errors should be on the cool side, for warmer temperatures will foster a stuffy and perhaps sleepy environment. As with any controls you can find, tape the thermostat controls to prevent tampering.

Light controls—Set the light controls to your taste. It is usually better to set room lighting to about 90% of full, which will create better intimacy and warmth for your speech. If you are planning to use any audiovisuals, check the lighting above the screen to ensure it does not reflect upon the screen and "wash out" your projection's image. And yes, tape down the switches after you have set them correctly.

If you need to have the lights adjusted, up or down, during your speech, mark the required settings on a piece of masking tape and ask an assistant to move the controls to those settings you marked earlier, at the appropriate time.

Clock—If there is a clock in the room, that is not located behind the audience, see if it can be removed. If it cannot be removed, perhaps you can arrange to have it neatly covered. Failing those options, ask to have it unplugged and set to 12 o'clock to remove the audience's temptation to watch it.

Windows—Any windows that may be in a room should have the curtains drawn closed, if their ambient light will affect any planned A/V or create a glare in the room. If uncovered windows must be accommodated, they are best at the back of the room, at the rear of the audience.

A/V equipment—If there were ever any devices that housed gremlins that can make things go wrong, they would be called A/V equipment. However, you can moderate and even eliminate most potential problems by testing any A/V you plan to use, *before you begin.* Test for correct operation, especially movie projectors. Make sure focus is sharp and that the image projected is square to the projector so there is no distortion. Set all A/V at the beginning point of their use, turn them off, and hope that the gremlins don't show up when you are ready to use them.

Extension cords—Safety of both your audience and yourself is the issue here. Ensure all extension cords and audio cables are taped down to prevent tripping.

Podium—The home of the "White Knuckle Speaker" requires an inspection prior to use. Often other meeting participants have "hid" items behind the podium for later use, and you don't want to knock them with your body and make noises, or have them fall out. In addition, for the same reasons, you should remove everything from the top of the podium that is not yours.

Water—Pitchers of water and glasses are often provided for the speakers, and you should if possible move them to a small table near, but not adjacent to the podium. You may wish to prepare one glass in advance for your potential use, and place it under the podium within easy reach.

Adding lemon to your prepared glass of water is an excellent technique to quickly cure a dry throat or wavering voice if you are unfortunate to suffer from either of those ills while speaking.

Microphone—There are fundamentally two choices when it comes to microphone selection, fixed or portable. Fixed will be podium or stand mounted, and if you are planning to be behind the podium, test its level to ensure it picks up your voice when you are in your planned speaking position. The optimum choice in most cases is the lavaliere wireless microphone. It gives you the most flexibility, but it also requires more thorough testing for audio levels and feedback, because with it you will be roaming around the stage and are therefore more prone to feedback situations.

ROOM LAYOUT

The physical layout of the chairs and tables in the room should be planned to your advantage, considering the effect of emotional focus. What you and your audience both want is to communicate. What you want is to diffuse emotional focus from the audience. Logically therefore you should select the room seating style that best helps you diffuse the audience's emotional focus.

There are three traditional ways to arrange seating in a room. They are classroom style, auditorium style (classroom style without tables), and "U" shaped. Although room and audience size may dictate which layout is best, you must try to select the room arrangement that helps you reduce your anxiety concerns.

Let's explore how and why different seating arrangements enable you to diffuse audience emotional focus. Picture yourself at the center of a circle of 100 people. They are standing shoulder to shoulder, and very importantly, they are facing away from you. With no one looking at you, you will not feel any emotional focus, and therefore you will not suffer from any anxiety. The 100 people in the circle are each looking at different places, and their aggregate emotional focus is diffused.

If you now looked through the special emotional focus camera that was available to you in Chapter 2, you would see lines radiating outward from the circle, each with a different focus point.

Next the 100 people turn around from the outward direction they were facing, and face inward. Guess where their lines of emotional focus will land. **On you!**

Guess if you would be more nervous if that happened than you did when they were looking away from you. You would! Obviously, the direction people face, in this example, makes a difference to the level of anxiety you sense and feel.

When it comes to selecting seating choices, the same premise applies. If you are trying to lessen their impact on you, and thereby reduce the threat of your "Tiger", seating choices that have the audience facing even slightly away from you are better than them facing directly at you. This fundamental principle should be considered and applied in your selection of an audience seating style.

(Although it may be tempting, for obvious reasons, it is not wise to seat your audience in a circle, facing away from you.)

CLASSROOM STYLE

The best seating arrangement of the traditional three styles, which will do the most to diffuse focus from you, is classroom style. Classroom style provides two clear advantages to the nervous speaker:

The first is rectangular seating (all seats facing forward in parallel). Preventing the powerfully intense emotional focus you "experienced" in the center of the circle a few paragraphs ago, by seating everyone in parallel seats diffuses the focus towards the center.

A second advantage of classroom seating is that further diffusion is gained by inserting a table between you and your audience. People will pay less attention to you if they are seated at a table, because they will focus elsewhere. They have more to look at than just you, and they will look at everything they can. They will look at their personal belongings, any notes they may take or even their tablemate or their tablemate's possessions. It's just the way people behave, and those on a "Tiger" hunt should use the situation to their best advantage.

Classroom seating is preferred as the seating tool to disperse focus from the speaker. It forces the bodies of the people in the audience to be directed away from where their eyes are focused. This puts the audience in a "weakened" position for potential group focus on the speaker. Less focus translates to less anxiety, and from a perspective of "White Knuckle Speaking" this is an important and a primary goal.

The point to remember, is that the more nervous you may be, the more reason there is to choose rectangular or "classroom" seating.

AUDIENCE STYLE

The next best alternative to classroom style seating is classroom style seating without the tables. This is called audience style.

From the perspective of a "White Knuckle" speaker, there is not a dramatic difference between classroom and audience style, but there is some. Obviously without the buffer of the tables you are subject to more intense emotional focus. Also there is a tendency in audience style for the chairs to be tilted towards you, and away from the rectangle.

As a matter of fact, as your confidence improves, you may wish to adjust the pure rectangular format of the room by tilting the rows from a perpendicular relationship to you the speaker, to one that may face you a little more. By "cheating" the rows to face you more directly, you will compromise some of the diffusion benefit, but you will improve your personal relationship with your audience and through that your overall effectiveness.

Audience style seating is the most standard seating option, and one with which you should become comfortable.

U-SHAPED STYLE

Having a similar affect on the speaker as the highly charged emotional focus circle, referred to earlier in this Chapter, the "U" shaped seating style should be avoided by the "White Knuckle" speaker.

The most intense focal point of this seating arrangement is at the center of the "U". This type of seating typically uses tables and is best for a relatively small group. There are situations, however, when group size, intimacy, and desire for group participation dictate that no tables are used. "U" style seating, however usually utilizes tables. Knowing this, "U" shaped seating presents both good and bad news to the novice.

The good news is that *only* the people at the far end of the tables will directly face you as you speak, and they are the farthest away. The remainder of the audience sits sideways to you, reducing the intensity of their focus on you, and a table buffers everybody from you. To those plotting to avoid emotional focus, these are two positive attributes.

The intensity at the center of the "U" is also a dangerous place, and its very presence should be avoided if you are not an experienced speaker. And now the bad news; because this type of arrangement is typically used for small groups, and because those on the sides will be craning to see and hear you, you will be drawn to the center as sure as a moth is drawn to a flame. However in your case there is no flame, just a "Tiger".

SEATING CHOICES

The alternative to indirect seating is more direct seating. In auditorium, classroom, and "U" shaped styles, all seating can be cocked on angles to face the podium or presenters location. Even "U" shaped arrangements can be opened up slightly to be less rectangular (approaching a semicircle), also with the objective to face the presenter.

The tradeoff you will have to make is between enhanced communications effectiveness through increased focus on you, and the desire to decrease your anxiety.

I recommend you take the focus and increased anxiety as much as you can, and hide behind a podium, using it as a shield until the butterflies die down. You however, are the better judge, not I. You will have to make the seating arrangement decision that is right for you. It will probably be based on the size of your "Tiger".

One final thought on room arrangements is that, if possible, you should not plan any excess seating. It is human nature that people will not sit in the first few rows. Attendees will tend to sit near the rear of the room, and if there are too many seats, a large empty space will appear quite awkward to both you and the audience. It is always better to plan for a few less attendees and add seats later if you need them.

A word of caution for you when you face the situation where "rear loaded" seating occurs; live with it. **Do not request the audience to move forward.** It is embarrassing for those that have to move, they probably won't move anyway, and as a result of your request, they will not be a warm, receptive audience.

A SPEAKER'S KIT

One idea, always valuable, and often invaluable, is to carry with you a speaker's kit. The kit is essentially a small satchel or bag in which you carry all of those things you may need to help you prepare for a successful speech. Your kit will be the repository for all of the special items you will need during your meeting room preparation activity. Items like masking tape and fresh felt tip pens are a requirement for room preparation, but anything is fair game as long as there is room.

You will find, over time, that many other clever items will find their way to your kit. Some examples are: a micro tape recorder to tape your speech, high energy snacks, a mechanical or laser pointer, change for the phone and other utilitarian items, such as paper clips, string, rubber bands, etc.

Also there are a number of personal items that you may find may be best carried in your speaker's kit. Consider items such as; cough drops, breath mints, Kleenex, an extra collar stay, or an emergency set of cufflinks. The contents of your kit bag will by definition be different from any other, but it is yours to manage, and you should pack whatever turns you on.

THREE SUMMARY THOUGHTS:

1. GO TO THE ROOM EARLY!
2. GO TO THE ROOM EARLY!
3. GO TO THE ROOM EARLY!

CHAPTER 9

▼

THE AUDIENCE

MAKE FRIENDS *BEFORE* YOU SPEAK

You are, of course, aware that you are never nervous or filled with anxiety when you are speaking with friends in your home, or with people you know during the business day. Also, after reading this far in this book, you are well aware why you are comfortable in front of friends and not comfortable in front of strangers. Therefore it is imperative that you do all you can to make friends of your audience before you speak. Building positive relations in this environment is a cakewalk compared to waiting until you enter the pressure filled speaking environment before you attempt to establish rapport.

MEETING AND GREETING

Shake hands, smile, and maintain eye contact. Those are the three basic tenets to successfully meeting and greeting people. And there is only one way to ensure you are effective at those three basic tenets; practice. Practice your handshake with a friend to get it firm and practice your smile and eye contact at the same time. Whenever you pass a mirror, check yourself out. Smile broadly and while looking at yourself, square in the eyes, introduce you to you in the mirror. You can never practice enough!

There are other things you can do to improve your meeting and greeting skills. The following are some ideas to help you, smoothly, along your way:

PREPARATION

1. Think through how you will introduce yourself to those you meet, and practice what you will say. You and your mirror will be able to polish this off in just a few minutes.

2. Check to ensure you have a good supply of business cards in your pocket.

3. Read the local newspaper. You will be amazed at how easy it is to make conversation, with the local knowledge you gained from this one activity.

PARTICIPATION

1. Use a name tag. Write big. Wear it high on your lapel.

2. Use the other person's name as frequently as possible in your conversation.

3. Ask questions of those you meet.

4. Be yourself, use humor if possible, but stay away from the jokes.

5. Move around to as many individuals or groups as possible. When you wish to end a conversation and go elsewhere in the room, just say, "Please excuse me", and leave.

FOUR DON'TS

1. Don't sit down!

2. Don't drink alcoholic beverages!

3. Don't be negative, about anything!

4. Don't tell jokes!

One additional thought to force conversation and help you establish positive relationships, is to wear a nametag or badge that says **"SPEAKER"**. It's the kind of thing you can keep in your speaker's kit, and in spite of its egocentric connotations, is a proven aide to building audience attention and rapport quickly.

My recommendation, for the most productive rapport building, is to seek out the audience's expectations with questions such as; What do you think the audience would like to hear tonight? The people you ask will be flattered and helpful, through the question you would establish your role as the speaker, and you will probably find information that you can weave into your remarks later that will demonstrate a sincere local connection with this audience.

Move around the group a lot, and make sure you find two or three people you might use as a "connection" at the beginning of your speech, for that is when you will need them the most. Their physical and emotional presence, as well as the potential to refer to them in the context of your speech is reason enough to seek them out. The specific advantages of utilizing audience members to assist you in diffusing emotional focus and taming your **"Tiger"** will be covered in greater detail later. Suffice for now that it will be to your advantage to find and cultivate two or three "friends", before you speak.

MANAGING THE "BATHTUB EFFECT"

Both the speaker and the audience begin all speeches with great anticipation. Both will expect a perfect liaison of words and mind from this speaking engagement, but it just doesn't work that way. In spite of your best efforts to plan and prepare for your speech there is a natural tendency for people to lose their focus and attention to the subject about one third of the way in.

This is fundamentally because human minds work three to four times faster than your voice appears in their ear. This natural phenomenon allows people to use brain cycles to store your message, compare it to prior thoughts or beliefs, and associate what it is hearing with personal experiences or planned activities.

An associate of mine once described this situation as the listener can use his or her brainpower to listen to you and dream of a vacation in Bermuda at the same time. "*The speaker's challenge*", he said, "*is to plan enough excitement in their speech to make them want to come back to hear more*".

This tendency to drift away in the middle of your speech is what I call the "bathtub effect". This term comes from the physical appearance of the audience's attention quotient if you plotted it on a graph.

It is up to the speaker to plan and plot his or her speech to keep bringing the audience back from Bermuda! In Chapter 5 the need to be creative was pointed out, now you can see the necessity. The **I-D-E-A** speech structure covered in Chapter 6 suggested communicating with examples to be effective. Both of these activities were focused right at this challenge of bringing them back.

You now have the structural tools to accomplish the task. The question to be answered is do you have the sincerity, the humor, the presence, and the grace to maintain your audience connection.

CONVEYANCE MANAGEMENT

Audience management is an activity that might be better identified as "conveyance management". It is working to most effectively convey your message, from you, to others in a public setting. Part of conveyance management is planning your speech using structural techniques to optimize your message. Another part is building rapport with your audience, to ensure a positive reception by them, which begins with meeting and greeting. The final area of conveyance management is the dynamics of audience involvement.

Many speeches, in which you include all of the ideas and techniques presented in this book, even when done well, still may lose their full effectiveness by lack of "connection" with the audience. This occurs when speakers only "address" or talk to an audience while failing to convey new ideas and opinions. The challenge is to get the audience to participate at all times.

Speaking effectively demands participation by the audience! The lion's share of audience participation will typically be intellectual, and therefore silence will reign except for your voice. However you can make this silence electric, first with their intellectual participation, then by asking rhetorical questions in the body of the speech, and then, if you have time, by seeking direct questions from the floor.

The object is for you to be effective by establishing and maintaining audience connection through eye contact and style. These actions will condition the audience to listen and learn. Managed to this state the audience will maintain an attitude of conveyance, and ideas and information will be able to flow freely from you to them.

ATTRIBUTES FOR CONVEYANCE

Audience participation of this type is difficult to achieve and takes much practice to attain regularly. However there are four attributes of successful conveyance that, if employed in your speech, will encourage active audience participation and therefore open to conveyance. These attributes should be considered in the development of your presentation. The four attributes are:

1. **QUESTIONS**—Be careful on this one! Apparently the most obvious means to obtain audience participation, it is not always so. The timing, manner and purpose of the question have much to do with the quality and usefulness of the answer. Questions, from you, should be pre-planned and structured to elicit genuine involvement (participation) rather than conventional response.

   Use informational questions during your deflection and diffusion period at the beginning of your speech. During the body of your remarks, use rhetorical questions to maintain involvement and personalization of your message. After you deliver your action statement, and if you have the inclination to answer direct questions from the audience, you may want to state that at the beginning of your remarks, or now as you wish.

2. **LISTENING**—A fine art, and as stated earlier, one skill for which we are poorly trained. At times you may receive questions from the audience. Seldom practiced when preparing for presentations, the trick is to listen first...before answering, and even exaggerate your listening posture and mannerisms. This compliments the person questioning and improves confidence in both the questioner and you.

Listening is the best way to avoid answering the "wrong" question, and it helps you to get beneath the words to understand what is really being asked.

3. **ANSWERING**—Usually a simple activity at which we all feel we excel. However, when presenting, your answering technique deserves special attention. The manner in which you answer, no less than the content of your answers, will affect the nature and extent of audience participation. Three common areas to avoid are: Answering too much. Answering too rapidly. Becoming trapped in a dialogue with only one person.

4. **CONTROL**—Maintaining control is essential, no matter how informal, active and keen the interchange may become. Different materials, the presentation, your own personality, all mix to create reactions to your statements. The challenge is to stimulate the reactions while maintaining your assumed role of group discussion leader.

Try to keep a minimum level of restraint, to keep the participation going. However this is a dangerous area, for you can easily lose control and even credibility with the manner in which you handle or answer questions.

Experience is the best teacher in this area, and I have found that a good way to learn good audience control techniques is to watch other presenters interact with their audience and take notes of their techniques. The more experienced you become, the more you can "loosen the reins".

The wonderful connection that is made between speaker and audience through conveyance management will not only assist you as an anxiety reducer in your desire to tame your "Tiger", but it will also assist the audience. With planning on you part the audience will improve their listening and learning, which will in turn improve your public speaking effectiveness.

THE "EYES" HAVE IT!

You can read it in this book or any of the other excellent books on public speaking or effective presentations to improve your ability, or you may learn it through your own experience, but the best place to learn it is in front of your mirror.

Look at yourself, you can easily inspect your overall looks and the impression you give to others, you have done it countless times before. However there is only one way to inspect and assess the impression you give to others of your sincerity. You have to look at yourself right in the eye!

The eyes are the primary tool humans use to communicate emotion and meaning. Your effectiveness, yes even your integrity will be judged in direct proportion to the amount of eye contact you maintain with your audience. If there is one critically important activity in any speech or presentation, it is to *MAINTAIN EYE CONTACT!!!* Maintaining good eye contact is the fundamental attribute of all successful presenters. Eye contact is important to establishing relationships with your audience and ensuring their active participation and attention. It is your audience's eye contact with you that causes speaker's fear. It is your eye contact with them that will convey your message to them with impact.

The anxiety felt at the beginning of a presentation makes eye contact difficult for the "White Knuckle Speaker". Inexperienced speakers sensing the intense focus of their audiences eyes riveting in on them will naturally shy away from establishing and maintaining eye contact. Their tendency is to look down at their notes, and once they do, they find it increasingly difficult to look up.

Solid eye contact, from you to your audience, will build their confidence in you. This confidence will help establish and bond a relationship between you and them that will enable their increased participation in you presentation. Perhaps through a nod, a smile, or even a look you will observe your audience joining with you in the presentation. Your eye contact to them will also allow you to assess their acceptance of your speech through their eye contact back to you.

When the connection is made between you and your audience; power, strength, and confidence will build rapidly within you. Your fears of the "Tiger" within you will be left behind, and you will be well on your way to the other end of the spectrum, and speaker's high!

DISTRACTIONS

Although audience distractions, such as crying babies, hecklers, noise from the next room, or the lawn mower outside your meeting room are rare, you should think through how you would handle these types of interruptions should they occur.

The best rule of thumb I can share with you is that distractions normally run their course and end relatively quickly. There is usually nothing you can do to stop the loud cougher in the room or the squealing brakes on the car outside. So your best course of action is to be just a bit patient, and let the extraneous distraction cure itself. The audience is as aware as you are to the distraction and if an audience member causes the distraction, they will help resolve it through "peer" pressure.

Distractions coming from outside your room will typically resolve themselves. If any of these types of cases continue to disturb you or your audience, I recommend you handle the disturbance by taking a small stretch break, until the distraction is remedied. You might say something like, "Let's take a brief five minute stretch break, until our friendly grass cutter moves on to the other side of the building."

A "heckler" or antagonistic audience member is a different case. Their behavior is destructive to your purpose, and must be remedied as soon as possible. Professional entertainers and political speakers typically deal with this type of distraction in a two-step approach. First they ignore the heckler and then if that does not work, they counterattack with a direct comment.

Comedians might say something like, "Did your mother have any children that lived?" I remember former President Ronald Reagan handling a heckler with a simple "Shut Up!" However, you probably aren't a stand-up comedian, or a professional politician, so I recommend a different two-step approach.

I have found the best way to handle a distracting audience interruption, is to first recognize the activity by stopping your remarks, thank the person for their question or comment and offer to discuss their subject after the close of your speech. (I often conveniently forget that commitment after the speech). If that action fails to stop the distraction, I advise you to look at the person that introduced you and ask them calmly for their assistance so you may proceed.

Dealing with the situation by using a mediator in this manner, keeps any potential conflict from you or your comments. The audience will thank you for your swift and appropriate handling of this distraction.

THREE SUMMARY THOUGHTS:

1.   Meet and greet three focus-diffusing "friends", before you speak.

2.   There are four attributes for gaining audience participation:
     - Questions
     - Listening
     - Answering
     - Maintaining control

3.   Distractions are rare, but they should be handled calmly and swiftly.

CHAPTER 10

▼

THE INNER YOU

I, like thousands of others, am inspired by the writings and speeches of Tony Robbins. He begins his book, "Awaken the Giant Within" with a quote from Orison Swett Marden; *"Deep within man dwell those slumbering powers; powers that would astonish him, that he never dreamed of possessing; forces that would revolutionize his life if aroused and put into action."*

I know of no quote that I have stumbled across in many decades of reading that more clearly sets out both the challenge and the potential of self-determination and the opportunity we all have to excel.

Throughout this book, the focus has been to build skills and techniques to meet and overcome speaker's fear. These tried and true techniques will help do the trick, but at the end of the day the question you must come to grips with is simple. **Can I do this?** The answer lies within your inner self, and only you have the answer. My belief is that you do have the ability to speak publicly without suffering the debilitation of speaker's fear. **It's time for you to believe that you can!**

Ron McKay stated, *"Deep within man dwell those slumbering powers; powers that would astonish him, that he never dreamed of possessing; forces that would revolutionize his life if aroused and put into action."*

A PUBLIC PERSON

Any speech, or presentation experience, presents you to others as a "public person". Becoming a public person and relating to others is both an internally rewarding and taxing experience. Over many years, you have learned how to be comfortable in dealing with others, typically in a one on one situation or a small group of only a few people.

Public speaking is a different experience, outside of your paradigm of "normal" communications expectations, but not one beyond your capabilities.

To some, being a "public person" is a virtually impossible task, for the potential trauma of speaker's fear far outweighs any perceived possible gain from the experience. This type of person is, at the worst extreme, a non-participant, or at the best, a classic "White Knuckle Speaker".

To others, who have learned to tame their "Tiger" of speaker's fear, the potential of becoming a "public person" is stimulating and offers the potential of a positive engagement with others. Those who learn how to correctly manage their inner self will demonstrate poise and become comfortable in the role of a public person.

CONTROLLING THOUGHTS

Did you ever wonder why in history, when a government is overthrown, the first thing the rebels took was the radio station. Why do you think a repressive or dictatorial government maintains state run newspapers and broadcast stations?

The reason is that they wish to control communications to the population. Those in charge of the communications can say or claim anything they want, including outlandish proclamations that may have no basis in truth, but with no opportunity for contradiction they may convince their listeners that what they broadcast is true. During World War II, Germany's Adolph Hitler controlled communications to an entire population through the artful skills of Dr. Goebbels, his propaganda minister and close personal associate.

Controlling communications controls thoughts. Controlling thoughts controls people. Through public speaking, like few other endeavors, you as an individual can control communications to a group. One can influence many with just the turn of a word, an innuendo of thought, and without so much as a scintilla of proof except one's own integrity and personal honor. It is up to you to be ethical, for the leverage of power you hold while communicating in front of others is great, and you must be your own ethical watchdog.

The speaking profession is constantly developing high standards and professional ethics to improve itself, through outstanding national organizations such as the National Speaker's Association (NSA). NSA members are jealous guardians of the current and future credibility of themselves and their professional reputation, and their efforts should be applauded and supported by every company and association that contract for a fee speaker.

At the end of the day, it is up to the individual speaker, at the time of their speech, to manage him or herself to high personal standards. In a nutshell the word is 'ethics'.

ETHICS

An anonymous quote states; *"In matters of the heart a charlatan cannot inspire others to what he himself does not believe."* Self-confidence, enthusiasm, excitement, all have integrity at their roots. To inspire an audience one must believe in their message, as a zealot would in their soul.

Speaking control, charisma, style, and inspiration, are manifestations of your beliefs. Of course you can and should vary tone, speed, level, pitch and other mechanical techniques to improve your speaking effectiveness, but without your sincere belief in what you are saying, it just won't work! What you do or say starts with who you are; your inner self. Nowhere else!

Vivian Buchan wrote in her book, Make Presentations with Confidence:

"Abraham Lincoln stood absolutely still, straight, and quiet. He never touched the podium, made wild gestures or walked around. On the other hand Theodore Roosevelt was a fiery, vital, and bombastic speaker who used his whole body as an instrument of expression."

That's where this subject of personal mastery comes to ground! You see you are you, and only you. You should strive to be the best you can be, and not something you are not. Therefore your best coach is your inner self. It's the person looking back at you from your mirror. Don't slough off the responsibility you have as a public speaker, and miss the grounding of your speaking skills in two words. **INTEGRITY** and **ETHICS**!!

POISE

The poised speaker appears self-confident and rightfully in command of the situation. Poise is a result of confidence. How you feel about you is the basic issue. It begins with your own confidence in your presentation preparation through structured preparation, it includes personal items such as how you dress, how you look, your energy, your posture, the impression you give to your audience, and many other items.

In Chapter Two (Understanding the Fear), it was pointed out that you have a personal "comfort zone", from which it is difficult to emerge. However, difficult or not, in public speaking there is a need for you to connect your private and public feelings through the buffer zone separating your private self (comfort zone) and your public self (public person). This connection will assist you to expand your personal comfort zone while becoming a more comfortable public person.

Education, experience and preparation are the action words to help you attain less anxiety and greater poise as a public person. How you feel about your inner self, and how you tame your "Tiger" is what this is all about.

What you are after is success. Building confidence in the "inner you", can lead to positive success.

THREE STEPS TO POSITIVE SUCCESS

STEP 1: *CLEAR YOUR HEAD!*

Complete your presentation more than 24 hours in advance. It can be two or twenty days in advance, but do not allow presentation work to encroach on your "prep" time. You will need a clear mind to focus on positive actions and tasks to best prepare for the big event.

Visit friends, play some golf, read a book, see a movie. Demonstrate to yourself that you ARE prepared. If you followed the suggested structure and techniques shared earlier in the 'PREPARATION NOT PERSPIRATION' section of this book you are as ready as you can be.

What Step I is doing is getting you to relax, so that your physical and mental energies will be heightened for the presentation. Know you're ready, relax through the day, and when you sleep, sleep the sleep of a winner.

STEP 2: *FOCUS IN!*

Approximately two hours before the scheduled speech or presentation, you must begin to get yourself focused. You know you have a well-prepared presentation, so review it lightly (5—10 minutes) to begin to be in touch with your message. You will not be particularly nervous at this time, so look in a mirror and make a few key remarks from your material in an animated or exaggerated manner. Smile! Enjoy!

Now that you know you and your material are ready, sit in a comfortable chair and start to visualize your audience. Try to imagine their interest and pleasure with your remarks, and yes if you can, their applause. Say your "A" or ACTION line of commitment to them, pause, say thank you aloud, and imagine their applause again.

In Step 2, you are beginning to connect your private self to your public self. Positive imaging will help reduce any anxiety. You know you will get an adrenaline rush just before you speak, and you are taking steps to handle it by building your confidence to meet it, and handle it. Step 2 ends with getting dressed or if dressed, freshening up, so you know you look good, and you know the audience will know you look good.

STEP 3: *GETTING UP!*

Music is my first choice. Carry a cassette tape and player of what music "turns you on" and play it loud an often, as you are getting dressed for your speech. It doesn't matter your musical style, but make it bold and you in turn will be the same.

Bob Richards, former Olympian gold medal winner and noted public speaker, drinks black coffee before he presents. One associate of mine walks briskly around the block before speaking.

Psychosomatic crescendo is what Step 3 is all about. Get yourself alert, excited and energetic. Figure out what works for you and do it!

Pilots preflight their equipment before they takeoff to ensure a successful flight. Taking care of and tuning your "inside" is the equivalent for you. Like Rocky Balboa, the fighter in the movie "Rocky", you will find that you too will become a champion by working at the fundamentals, by tending to the basics, and preparing your mind and body to succeed, before the "fight"…getting stronger everyday….

What activities you settle on to do in the above Three Steps to Success, are your personal choice. There is no "right" way. Get comfortable with yourself, your attitude and the inner you.

MIRROR MIRROR

Practice! Practice! Practice! And where best to practice with privacy, and no emotional pressure, but alone in front of a mirror. Ballerinas practice for hours on end in front of mirrors in a never-ending quest to master their profession. They work over great periods of time, on finite techniques and almost imperceptible movements that combine to present the excellence of grace to their audience.

You too will benefit greatly from the use of a mirror in practice. And like the ballerinas, you can use a mirror to work on the finer points of speaking, developing yourself towards personal speaking mastery.

The subject of personal mastery is worthy of some thoughtful repose, for if there ever was a subject, in this broad plethora of public speaking considerations, worthy of your undivided attention, it would be headlined under the professional act of personal mastery. Look at the person looking back at you in your mirror. Are you proud of what you see? The inner you will dominate the outer you. Get square with yourself, and you will be square with others. Look deeply and critically at yourself in the mirror and work to make yourself the best that you can be.

You and your mirror will work together to improve your speaking techniques and capabilities. And the cardinal lesson you will learn is, to be at ease and be natural. Listen to others suggestions to help you improve your stage presence. However don't become mechanical or unnatural in your actions. You must remain comfortable and natural and feel at home on the platform.

The speaker who is at home on the platform exudes confidence, and confidence is the font of charisma. Charisma is that power from within that overwhelms others with its engaging energy. Charisma and confidence is what will make you as a speaker appealing, admired, and remembered.

FOUR SUCCESS TRAITS

There is no one formula for good public speaking that is right for everyone. However, as you prepare for your next speech you will select the most appropriate tools, actions and techniques that will eliminate your nervousness, and optimize your effectiveness. Preparation for eliminating speaker's fear in your speech will be personalized and unique. There are, however, four generally common traits of successful speakers and they can be practiced in front of a mirror.

The four success traits are:

1. *EYE CONTACT*—This is the most important of the four traits. You must look at your audience, not beyond them. Eye contact itself helps hold attention and increase command. In turn the eyes of the audience will give you many clues to help you adapt yourself each moment to their needs. You will soon find yourself adapting readily to their needs as your speech proceeds.

   When practicing your speech, utilize the mirror to validate your eye contact to three major segments of your audience. Practice looking at the left, right and center sections of your audience approximately five or six rows deep. Due to your distance from the audience, this technique will give the audience the appearance that you are looking at each of them.

   Do not flicker your eyes around the room; spend two to three sentences at each of the three audience segments, for maximum impact.

2. *COMMAND*—The audience must realize there is someone of authority before them; the authority of the speaker, backed by the authority of his/her competence, sincerity and integrity. Basic to this is your ability to "project". There is authority granted to you because you are the speaker, and that authority is yours to lose by poor preparation.

Personal impact from your attire and your posture, have a significant impact to your ability to maintain command of the situation. Your mirror can obviously assist you in working on your posture and assessing if your clothing selection sends the message you need to send.

3. *VOICE*—Rule number one is that you must be heard! Your rehearsals and presentation development should include a cassette recording that you and a friend listen to, together. Listen to how you can better use your voice for variety, pace, interest, emphasis, and most importantly, projection.

   There are several books, which you should review, to improve your voice pitch and tone for public speaking. One book I would recommend, which I have found to be particularly helpful is "Change Your Voice, Change Your Life.", by Dr. Mort Cooper. Macmillan Publicity, New York, 1984. With this book and your mirror, can spend valuable time reviewing your voice and its potential impact.

4. *MOVEMENT AND GESTURES*—Perhaps the most dangerous areas of speaking technique, are movements or gestures. They are powerful if used correctly, and deadly if they appear contrived or distractive. All of your movements during a presentation should be conscious and deliberate, such as those of an actor. Observing them in front of your mirror will provide you a good impression of the impact of your movements.

   Moving out from behind the safety of the podium exposes more of you to the intensity of the audience, if you are well prepared, you can capture their attention and their minds with well orchestrated movement.

   Movement can help you control your presentation by relaxing you and shifting attention to you for important points that can be made most effectively. Judiciously chosen gestures can also help, however to most beginning speakers, they are difficult to pull off, without appearing to be too mechanical, or false.

Suffice it to say that your natural body rhythms are sufficient and the natural way to communicate change of mood or presentation emphasis. Use your normal gestures and movements whenever you can, for your natural personality will show through with sincerity and not falseness.

As your personal confidence builds, you may want to venture from behind the podium and then perhaps into the audience for even more impact or emphasis. However this technique in turn, puts increased focus on you from the audience, and with that increased focus you risk another round of adrenaline pumping through you for which you should be prepared to handle.

Therefore my counsel is to save this technique until you have better mastered control of your fears of presenting to people.

These four traits can be assessed and practiced in front of your mirror. Your mirror will be a silent partner in helping you to see yourself in action, during your continuing efforts to improve your speaking abilities. The watchword is practice…the benefactor will be you.

GESTURES & DISTRACTIONS

You, I'm sure, are aware not to jingle coins in your pocket, or twist a necklace, or pull your ear, scratch, bob your head, or rock back and forth while you speak. A few minutes in front of a mirror or video camera will quickly point out to you any obvious, repeating deficiencies you may have. You might also ask a friend to help critique you in a practice-speaking situation.

The point is to practice to minimize personal mannerisms that will distract from your message.

Gestures that can positively affect your message should be planned into your presentation and practiced. They should be planned to complement your message and not be viewed as obvious arm waving or pointing.

PRINCIPLES TO HELP

To help you plan gestures, apply the following principles:

1. Gestures must be in concert with tone of your message. You don't want to gesture and distract from your presentation.

2. Two gestures are considered "safe" in most presentations, and they are a vertical chopping or pointing action with your hand…and a broad sweeping move with your arm. These both appear "natural" to most speakers and should be considered for use when desired for either specific or general emphasis.

3. The planned timing of these or other gestures in your presentation should come as a result of verbal practices in front of a mirror, and marked in your practice script in the margin, *before* the word or phrase you wish to emphasize, and again at the word. I recommend a color highlight pen be used to cue you at the right moment, your eye will pick up the color easily and the rest will be easy.

A POSITIVE MENTAL ATTITUDE (PMA)

Dream it and you will become it! I believe in the strong connection of the will of the mind and the performance body referred to as, Psycho-soma, (Psycho—Mind; Soma—Body). Some days you get the "Tiger", and some days the "Tiger" gets you! But it doesn't have to be that way, you can get that "Tiger" any day you want to, if you believe you can. Maintaining a Positive Mental Attitude (PMA) in virtually everything you do assures, and almost insures success. In public speaking, it is essential.

Why is it you are comfortable speaking to a group of five year olds, and not the same number of adults? Because you feel that you will be able to easily handle any situation or subject that occurs. If you are the "expert" relative to any group you speak to, you will have confidence and minimal fear. If you are prepared, and you have planned deflection and diffusion techniques, you will be the "expert", relative to your audience. Developing a Positive Mental Attitude (PMA) is the first step. *Mastering your attitude is the key!*

An introspective look at your inner self, to help you come to grips with the concept that you can and will be successful, as a public speaker, is an important step for you to make. Most, who fail in any endeavor, do so because they begin their quest with the fundamental belief that they will not succeed. Those that typically succeed do just the opposite. As you strive to improve your speaking skills and reduce or even eliminate speaker's fear, it is best to believe in yourself and your ultimate success. Look in your mirror, and see a winner!

PMA WORKS!

Famous pro golfer Chi Chi Rodriguez was practicing for a tournament at a golf ourse at which I used to be a member. The course was not in its best condition, due to an unusually dry summer and other pros were complaining loudly and frequently of the "poor shape" the course was in.

When asked how he liked the course and its condition Chi Chi responded, *"This is the best course I have ever played, it is in wonderful shape!"* He later explained he took that position at every course he played because he believed a positive approach (PMA) to his game reduced anxiety, and allowed his physical skills to be loose and natural, enabling him to perform at his best.

Like Chi Chi, both physical and mental preparation is obviously important to your success. Being fully prepared both "inside" and "outside" will remove anxiety and fear from your presentation. Not understanding what to do to best prepare yourself both "outside and inside, will only lead to "White Knuckle Speaking"!

Dr. Norman Vincent Peale speaks of Mario Lanza suffering such terrorizing stage fright, every time he performed, that he was unable to walk out and face the audience without an unusual personal activity. Mario Lanza knew of his musical genius, and so he would "look at himself in a mirror", acknowledge to himself that he would be successful yet again (PMA), and then recognizing that his stage fright was superficial to his innermost feelings, he would banish it!

He would yell at himself, "*Get Out, Little Me!!*", banishing the part of him that was afraid and allowing his "*Big Me*" to perform not only comfortably, but beautifully to the delight of his audience. His approach may have been eccentric, but his Positive Mental Attitude allowed his audience to enjoy the benefit of his mastery of music.

When asked why he did not become frustrated and give up his quest for a functional electric light bulb, Thomas Edison responded: "*I learned 191 ways that a light bulb would not work, before I found one that did.*". In pursuit of his signature invention, it would have been easy to give up after 30-40 attempts, or even after 75 or 100, especially if he viewed those attempts as failures.

Thomas Edison considered every attempt at discovery, a learning experience, and not a failure. His positive mental attitude (PMA) is why he continued on diligently time and time again. Would you venture a guess at our civilization's progress without his persistent attitude?

LIFE TAPES

Professionals have written volumes about our "life tapes." Earlier in Chapter Two, they were discussed in detail. These "tapes" dictate our current behavior, by acting as our memory bank allowing us to choose our next actions relative to our past experiences.

The basics of your PMA were formed during that period of your life. When you are asked to stand in front of others and speak, you check our "tapes", determine that you will be operating outside our comfort zone and realize that you will be exposed to potential embarrassment. Even before you actually present in front of a group you become apprehensive; you can sense your hands moving slowly toward your throat for the "big choke".

Offsetting this potential disaster when speaking in front of a group is what this book is all about. Knowing that you are prepared with excellent structure, anxiety defeating tools and effective speaking techniques will provide you the basis for banishing your fears, as did Mario Lanza.

Jack Lemon, noted actor, said; *"Without heightened apprehension, an actor probably won't give as good a performance as he should."* There's nothing wrong with a little personal excitement, fueled by apprehension, to get you "up" and going. With a positive mental attitude, you can convert that apprehension to speaking excellence.

PRE-SPEECH ROUTINE

Dumbo believed he could not fly, in spite of his natural "gift". You will recall that Dumbo's friend and associate, Timothy the mouse, presented Dumbo with a "magic" feather, and assured him that if he grasped it in his trunk, before he launched off the stand at the top of the circus tent, that he could fly.

From that moment on, Dumbo knew he could fly, **assuming** he followed his preflight routine each and every time he wanted to fly.

Professional athletes develop and adhere religiously to a pre-event routine that they repeat in preparation for success each time they act. It may be pre-fight, pre-match or pre-game, or even pre-speech, but the preparation helps.

In your case you need to develop a repeatable pre-presentation regimen that will deliver you to the beginning of your presentation, "ready to go", with no inhibitions to slow you down, just the knowledge that there is nothing more you can do to get ready, and all you have to do is execute.

Pro golf legend Jack Nicklaus has stated that he will not begin any round of golf without three and only three pennies in his pocket. Some may attribute this to superstition, but that is not the issue. The issue is that for whatever reason he repeats the same set of actions before each round, just as a pilot will preflight his or her aircraft, in a specific order before the plane takes off. The mental confidence that all is prepared, provides a base of confidence that allows the individual to focus on what will happen, not what should have happened.

Think through what your "pre-speech routine" should be. Keep it simple, and repeatable. You will find that a consistent routine will assist you to reduce anxiety and your tendency to be a "White Knuckle Speaker".

THE POINT OF NO RETURN

At the end of your preflight routine, you have symbolically reached the point of no return. Success awaits you, as it awaited Dumbo, however it is dependent upon you.

Dave McNally wrote in "Even Eagles Need a Push", "*The eagle drew courage from an innate wisdom. Until her children discovered their wings, there was no purpose for their lives. Until they learned how to soar, they will fail to understand the privilege it was to have been born an eagle. The push was the greatest gift she had to offer. It was her supreme act of love. And one by one she pushed them, and they flew.*"

It's time for you to fly.

THREE SUMMARY THOUGHTS:

1. What you say is the manifestation of your beliefs. What you do or say starts and ends with who you are; your inner self.

2. There are three steps to Positive Success, which you should consider as you prepare yourself for your speaking engagement:
    *   Clearing your head.
    *   Focusing in.
    *   Getting yourself up!

3. Think through what your "pre-speech routine" should be. Keep it simple, and repeatable. You will find that a consistent routine will assist you to reduce anxiety and your tendency to be a "White Knuckle Speaker".

▼

PART FOUR

IT'S SHOWTIME!

A TRAINED TIGER IS A WONDERFUL PET

CHAPTER 11

THE OUTER YOU

CLOTHES

True or False? Clothes make the speaker! Well, they sure don't hurt, and as a matter of fact, they are a major part of the impression you leave wherever you go. You know everyone including yourself makes judgments about people from first impressions.

For example, when you see someone in church, or at the airport, or at the supermarket, you form an impression of him or her. From what? From their total persona, but dominantly from how they look, and that decision is probably made from what they are wearing. As a presenter, with all of those eyes focused on you, you will want to use what you wear as a tool to establish rapport, give a positive impression and communicate confidence.

In his book "I Can See You Naked", Ron Hoff makes some important points on this subject. He states: "*What you wear, when making a presentation, is one of the strongest components of what you communicate. Here's why:*

Your clothes, or more specifically, what you choose to wear when presenting, are pure nonverbal communication. Clothes communicate almost instantaneously, as quickly as the eye can telegraph a snapshot to the mind. Clothes provide a self-portrait of you. You are what you wear.

Fashion has drummed this concept into our minds—and it has gained a certain credibility. Clothes are universal. Everybody wears them. Outside of a nudist camp, you won't find many audiences totally disregarding the importance of clothes. Thus, you can't dismiss or pooh-pooh the relevance of clothes to your presentation effectiveness. They're very important.

What you wear tells us, your audience two fundamental things: Your perception of YOURSELF. Your perception of US."

Pay special attention to selecting your clothes for your speaking engagement.

The "Buttoned Down" Look

After over a quarter century of business experience within the traditionally conservative I.B.M. Corporation, you would probably be able to recognize me as I entered the door by my "look". I remember my daughter describing my clothing selection, as "*early nerd*".

Some may kindly guess me, as I enter the room, to be a banker, an FBI agent, or even an undertaker. You can conjure up the image I am relating to: Dark pin striped suit, red striped tie, white (buttoned downed) shirt, black wing-tipped shoes.

Why do you think this conservative "dress code" was sustained in I.B.M. and other major companies for many years? **Because it WORKED!**

The identification of conservative dress with I.B.M. was a consistent and critical factor in the customer's choice to do business with I.B.M. versus other companies. There is no great secret as to why using conservative dress, as a communicator of company image was successful.

Dressing in the same genre as customer executives, financial managers and company presidents, assists in establishing both relationships and an effective communications environment with those individuals who are the key business decision makers.

A conclusion may be drawn, when you are to speak in front of an audience, that if you dress at or near the standards of your audience, you have taken a positive step towards acceptance. My personal views is that you should always plan your attire to match or exceed that of your audience, but never appear dressed below their standards.

Let's look at that more closely. Dressing within the range of your audience is an effective tool to establish relationships and effective communications. It is obvious, but probably worth stating that dressing below the range of your audience is not constructive, and it will only add to your personal anxiety and the potential for "White Knuckle Speaking".

In a business environment you will usually know what "normal" business attire for your presentation is. It is more difficult to ascertain that for other presentation events, such as civic, club or association activities, however there is always someone to call to ascertain the expected level of dress. The task then is to determine the expected attire of the audience and plan your wardrobe in advance.

A fear reducing technique I have found particularly helpful, is that after determining what I will wear at the presentation at least a week in advance, I have my selected suit, shirt, etc. cleaned, my shoes shined and then I store all of it in my closet, ready for me on the "big day". You would be amazed at the power and comfort you feel, preparing for your presentation with this approach, knowing you are ready. It is similar to preparing for a "big date", with the anticipation and excitement leading towards the event, personally stimulating.

Early selection and preparation of your clothes for this occasion will help control your anxiety by giving you improved confidence that this area of your planning was well completed. Look in a mirror, if you like yourself, you *know* you audience will like you.

Again to quote from Ron Hoff, in "I Can See You Naked": "*Clothes don't just cover, they communicate. They don't just protect you they project you. They showcase your perception of yourself.*"

What about the other half of the equation? What about your perception of them—the people out there in the audience? What do your clothes say about your feelings towards them? The answer is short and simple. It is so unsophisticated that it probably predates the invention of fashion. "*We tend to like people who, on special occasions, get a little dressed up for us. Nothing splashy. Nothing flashy. 'Just a little bit' dressed up.*"

GROOMING

I don't know about you, but it never fails that when I am working at home on the weekend, I need something from the store to complete the job. In work clothes, typically unshaven, with hair disheveled. I trundle to the store, and typically receive a different level of service than I am accustomed to. I become frustrated by the fact that I do not receive the same level of service that I would were I to stop by the same store during the week. Is this because it is the weekend, or is it possible that my image is different because of my poor grooming? I believe the latter.

Let's face it. Everything counts! You are responsible for the presentation of yourself in both your personal and business world. As a speaker you have a special responsibility to present a well-groomed figure. As a rule of thumb, women speakers tend to display consistently good taste in both the style and color coordination of their clothing selection, so allow me a brief discourse on the clothing selections made by men.

Remember, the issue here is to prevent personal embarrassment, to minimize anxiety, and reduce speaker's fear. The guideline to follow for both men and women is conservative attire, with suits, (not sport coats) of dark blue or gray, without strong patterns in the material.

John T. Molloy, in his book "The New Dress for Success", focuses strongly on the role and impact of a man's tie. He addresses, "*How to pick your most important status symbol, your tie"*. He explores the ramifications of correct tie selection in depth, and ends with the following statement, which I feel demonstrates the significance of correct tie selection. *"Show me a man's ties, and I'll show you who he is trying to be."*

Often I am asked about whether certain types of facial hair, glasses, hairstyles, etc. are appropriate. Even King Solomon would be challenged to answer those questions correctly. The answer is unique to the individual, and what is good for the goose is not necessarily good for the gander. As a speaker, the guiding principle in these matters rests not with you. You are not the judge. The judge is the person who is in charge of the meeting, the one who signs the checks, and it is totally appropriate to ask him or her how you should dress.

Let me share with you a word to the wise in this important matter. Several years ago, at one of my first speaking engagements, I was unsure of the dress standard for the event I was addressing, so I thought I would take my cue from the people with whom I was working, leading up to the event. They were bright, always casually dressed, "arty" people, and I assumed I would be perfectly safe dressed that evening in a business suit. I was safe, however just a little out of place at the "Black Tie Affair".

If all else fails and you have to guess the correct grooming or attire for you, default to the "employment model". In other words, every time you wonder if you are appropriately groomed, assume you are going for an employment interview with the company to whom you're presenting. If you pass muster with yourself, then you probably have it right. Only you and your mirror can answer the question correctly. If you remain unsure, ask a close friend for areas of grooming in which you can improve.

Stealing a line from an old Gillette razor ad. Look *Sharp!…. Feel Sharp!…. Be Sharp!*

WEIGHT

My thoughts on this personally sensitive area can best be communicated with the help of an old joke. A 5'3" tall man, weighing over 350 pounds, entered a men's clothing store seeking a new suit for a very important date he had that evening. The clerk inquired, "Are you looking for anything special?" To which the man answered, "I want the Carey Grant look in a 56 stout!"

Some things are just not meant to be!

You are what you are, and I do not presume to judge your total physical presentation. I recognize there is no magic formula to presenting a professional image, but common sense tells us that an energetic, in shape, vibrant speaker has an positive impact advantage over those who do not display those characteristics. Those characteristics should be your goal.

YOU ARE ON DISPLAY

The "outer" you is what is on display to others. Personal pride and commitment to putting your best foot forward is imperative in developing a lasting professional image, and becoming an effective public speaker. It is also critically important to your own self-esteem, which you need to remain strong to help fight speaker's fear.

There is a difference in being fit and being healthy. I like many others was shocked at the surprising death of leading American distance runner, Jim Fixx. How could someone with world class running skills suffer a heart attack while running? Is it possible that he was fit, but not healthy? I do not profess an expertise in health or fitness, but I strongly recommend you work closely with medical professionals to become the best you can be.

Let me assure you that public speaking is both emotionally and physically draining. At the close of a day in which I speak, I am *drained!* As if in an athletic contest I find that my personal commitment and involvement cause me to give my all. To be an energetic public speaker you must be fit. Diet, exercise, and a positive mental attitude, are all areas of personal health that you should maximize.

THE FINAL ANALYSIS

As a public speaker, it is you that will be judged for your total presentation. As an individual you can rationalize any component of the impression you leave, but as a speaker, excuses or explanations after the fact will not help anything. Besides personal considerations, you should pay attention to not using obscene or offensive language, staying away from drinking alcoholic beverages, and while socializing be as charming as possible to any guest at the event.

The challenge is that, in this case, in the final analysis, you are not the final arbiter, your audience is. Do your best!

THREE SUMMARY THOUGHTS:

1. Clothes communicate. They don't just protect you they project you. They showcase your perception of yourself."

2. Always match or exceed your audience's level of dress.

3. Look Sharp…Feel Sharp…Be Sharp!

CHAPTER 12

▼

PUTTING IT ALL TOGETHER

LET THE GAMES BEGIN!

You are now at commencement, the beginning of successful speaking, without, "*White Knuckles*"! You know how to tame your "Tiger. You understand and can use the **I-D-E-A** speaking structure. You have enough information explaining the "What, Why, and How" of effective public speaking and you are ready to put "*White Knuckle*" speaking behind you for good.

Key to your comfort is your understanding that "speaker's fear" is normal, but you now have the tools to counteract that fear and deal successfully with your personal "moment of truth". All that is left for you is the plunge, and although the plunge will seem insurmountable, I assure you it will be easily handled because you are prepared for it.

MURPHY'S LAW FOR SPEAKERS

Most are satisfied with utilizing "Murphy's Law" as an excuse for things that go wrong. You know; "Whatever can go wrong, will go wrong."

You however can ensure that things will go right for you if you consider this extension to "Murphy's Law". "Whatever can go wrong, will go wrong; *therefore you should anticipate it, and prepare for it, so that you will succeed.*" Consider the entire statement when you are getting it all together for a successful speech. Because you anticipate potential "White Knuckle Speaking" problems, you can plan, prepare and practice to tame your "Tiger". You are as ready as you will ever be, so it's time to get on with it.

THE NIGHT BEFORE

The day of the speech actually starts the night before. Try to spend that evening relaxed, without any cramming for the big event. You might consider taking a relaxing walk, seeing a movie or reading that book you've always wanted to read. Choose whatever activities suit you, but remember the purpose of these activities is to help you get a good night's sleep.

If you aren't well rested on the day of your speech, you just won't do as well as you could. So take a night off from everything but relaxations, knowing you are as ready as you can be, and sleep the sleep of a winner.

EARLY TO RISE

Ahh! the morning. Arise early, read the paper, have a little breakfast, exercise or at least indulge in a brisk walk, and you're ready to go. Do whatever you want to do to "get up" for the day!

- Listen to your favorite music!
- Get positive!
- Talk to yourself about how good this day will be!
- Rev up that P.M.A.!

Between the time you arise and the time you arrive at the site of your speech, you will want to quickly run through your speech with your friend in the mirror at least once more. Organize yourself, get dressed, and make that last run-through before you leave. Before you go, take that last look in the mirror, smile, and wish yourself luck.

Leave with plenty of time to check out the meeting room. When you arrive, begin your pre-speech routine. Whatever routine you have decided to do to sequence you towards meeting and greeting your audience should be done, as soon as you arrive.

It is strongly recommended that you end your personal pre-speech routine at the meeting site, by greeting your "Tiger", and informing him that he need not show up today, because everything is well prepared. Now that you have learned how to train him, the time is *now* to put him in his cage! Tell him to waltz right in!

Begin to concentrate on the big moment ahead. You may be thinking of the butterflies, the sweaty palms, the need to grip the podium tightly...the *"White Knuckles"*. But remember, you have trained your "Tiger", and these feelings will just be fleeting. What you should be focused on is just three things:

1. Your material
2. Yourself
3. Your Audience

YOUR MATERIAL

Review in your mind the four structural items in your presentation. Your **INTRODUCTION...DRAWING** them **IN**...the **EXAMPLES** you will use, and then the **ACTION** you wish them to take.

Rehearse your memorized Introduction and Drawing in sentences. There will only be three or four of them and they, combined with the deflection or diffusion techniques you have selected, will carry you across the "speaker's fear moment of truth" you will face during the first minute of anxiety. Your planned deflection and diffusion techniques will help you through the remainder of your *"White Knuckle"* time, after which you will be coasting down the adrenaline slide to a well prepared, successful presentation.

Quickly review the Examples you plan to cover and visualize your audience listening to you and nodding in agreement. Rehearse your Action statement sentence, and as suggested earlier, write it down somewhere that you will see it easily in the final rush of the speaker's high.

YOURSELF

First things first. Make sure your host has the proper introduction for you, and that he/she knows how to correctly pronounce your name. An error by your host in you introduction carries over to you. Help yourself start smoothly by helping your host get it right the first time.

Always bring with you, a copy of the introduction you prepared for the host to introduce you (The host will invariably forget his or her copy). Unless you are blessed with a "John Smith" name, go over the pronunciation of your name one last time.

Review all of the room arrangements, and then go to the front of the room. Sit in your seat for a few seconds, and get a sense of your surroundings, walk up to the podium and look around from there. Then speak your **I** and **D** sentences to get a feeling for what it will feel like when you actually begin.

Finally, check out your personal appearance, one last time. Once everything is in its right place, pronounce you are ready and go out to meet your audience.

YOUR AUDIENCE

The audience's arrival marks the beginning of your speech. Anything, and everything, you can do to establish a positive relationship with them, will assist you in both reducing speaker's fear and delivering an effective speech.

Attendees will want to meet you, and obviously you will want to meet them, so utilize the information given in Chapter Nine, about how to smoothly meet and greet your audience.

Also remember to find a "friend" or two to help you across the emotional stress of "White Knuckle Speaking", when you first begin. Lastly, flow into the meeting room with the audience and move to your pre-arranged seat.

THE BRIDGE

I call the period of time from when you stop socializing with your audience until you speak as "the bridge". As a bridge it spans the transition between the two events and allows you to personally "shift your communications gears" from general conversation to public speaking.

One of my favorite techniques for reducing personal anxiety immediately before a presentation is to stand as long as possible before you must sit and the program begins.

While standing, turn and overlook the audience to extract some of their first reactions. You will find a few smiles and encouraging nods that if you respond to with confidence will help you build audience rapport even before you speak. Look for your "friends", they will enjoy the recognition and you will benefit from the early connection.

The poise you demonstrate during the "bridge" will pay off handsomely when you begin to present.

RELAX

Start by calming your thoughts. You are fully prepared for your speech. You have deflection and diffusion techniques planned. You have designed a winning speech structure, utilizing **I-D-E-A**. There is nothing more you can do now, except to calm down, and manage the "Tiger".

In the few minutes before you speak, it is important to keep the upper hand with your "Tiger" to minimize your anxiety and prevent a severe case of "White Knuckle Speaking". It is time to maintain control of the situation by remaining calm and in control.

Physical exercise will condition both your body and mind to relax. Given you can't go to the gym for a workout, you need to learn a few isometric exercises to employ while you are awaiting your introduction.

Exercise 1: Press your hands together firmly, for about ten seconds and repeat five times.

Exercise 2: Repeat the prior exercise substituting your knees instead of your hands. As an added twist, while pressing your knees together, try pressing your feet to the floor.

Exercise 3: Beginning at the small of your back and continuing upward, roll your spine forward while holding your chin down firmly against your neck.

Remember, that you will probably feel surges of speaker's fear float by as you wait. This are natural feelings, so don't be overly concerned. If it happens, just concentrate on your next exercise and take a few deep breaths. Deep breaths will help, but you should continue the isometrics, because together they will both consume the extra adrenaline coursing through your body, as a result of any building anxiety, and they will act as a purposeful divergent for your mind, until your introduction.

When you hear the moderator begin your introduction, your anxiety will begin to obviously increase. Don't worry, because this is again a very natural reaction to the situation. As a matter of fact, the surge of adrenaline you begin to feel at this time is good, for it will feed your energy level for the beginning of your speech. Welcome the power your body is providing you, at this important moment. Drink it in!

EXPLODE!!

When you hear the final word of your introduction, spring forward towards the moderator to shake their hand and thank them profusely for their introduction. Be energetic, be forceful, and be excited!

Turn to your audience and smile! Wave at your "friends"! The abundant energy, built up by your adrenaline, will help you "connect" to the audience, and it will be contagious to them.

BE BOLD

"Be bold; and mighty forces will come to your aid." The mighty forces are within you and they await their call to arms. Who has not faced fearful situations, against which you simply forged ahead and found success.

Boldness is a deliberate decision to participate in a manner different to our experience.

The difference between actions of boldness and our normal state creates tension within us. This tension (fear) typically stops us from challenging the unknown. Fear is the most paralyzing of all emotions.

At this "moment of truth" you must simply plunge ahead and trust your newfound abilities to sustain you. Your natural skills and instincts will take care of you. Like a baby learning to walk, or a young child learning to swim, the moment of fear is easily offset by the thrill of success. The time will fly by. You will stay on track because of the **I-D-E-A** structure with which you planned your speech.

Pause for a moment while you recall your "I" and "D" statements. Slowly look over your audience, smile the biggest smile of your life, and begin.

But a word of caution is appropriate here. A common error of less experienced speakers, who recently have overcome "White Knuckle Speaking", is to get caught up in the euphoria of their success. Many will lose their way, and either forget or run right by their closing statements. The adrenaline, that caused speaker's fear in the first place, is now a positive rush of energy that many find difficult to turn off. This is why a pre-planned "A" statement is most effective, and required.

PAUSE BEFORE YOU CLOSE

When your last "Example" is given, pause. Take a deep breath, look squarely at the audience, and slowly lay that big "A" on them. The "*ACTION*" statement is what you wanted them to do; it's the purpose of your speech. Give it to them right between the eyes, and then pause a second time.

Say "Thank you", then return directly to your seat. From this moment on, the excitement is yours to enjoy. Sit down and get ready to enjoy that well earned emotional rush called "speaker's high" that I referred to at the beginning of the book.

There is no way I could ever explain the deep feeling of the speaker's high you will experience when you sit down at the end of your speech. It's a more powerful emotional feeling than speaker's fear, only it's positive. There is nothing like it!

THE END

And now I would like to commit you to some Action. Whatever your speaking skills were, as you began this book, I believe they have now changed. I would like you to identify the two most beneficial ideas or techniques that you have learned from this book, write them down, and use them the next time you have an opportunity to speak in public.

Can you remember the adage I used at the beginning of this book, "Sometimes you get the 'Tiger', and sometimes he gets you." Because you now know how to train him, from this time forward, when you confront your "Tiger" you will be able to "make him dance". He'll never get you again.

"White Knuckle Speaking" is behind you! *CELEBRATE!!*

THREE SUMMARY THOUGHTS:

1. Complete your preparation the day before.

2. Cross over the "bridge".

3. *CELEBRATE!*

ABOUT THE AUTHOR

Andy Ruppanner

Throughout his 30 years of executive business experience with IBM and Office Depot, and as an entrepreneur founder of several technology companies, Andy has developed and applied his skills as a visionary public speaker and strategist to the benefit of his companies, clients, and community.

An MBA from Emory University, Andy is an exciting leadership speaker of national reputation, and the recipient of many significant awards for managerial excellence and community service.

A "patriot" for business in America, Andy is committed to the premise that business leadership is the preferred agent for accomplishing positive change and stability in our society.

Andy Ruppanner may be contacted via his website at *www.ruppanner.com.*

BIBLIOGRAPHY

Awaken the Giant Within, by Anthony Robbins. Simon & Schuster; New York, New York. 1991.

Effective Business and Technical Presentations, by George L. Morrisey. MOR Associates, Addison-Wesley; Reading, Massachusetts. 1986

Even Eagles Need a Push, by David McNally. Delacorte Press; New York, New York. 1971.

Future Edge, by Joel Barker. William Morrow & Co.; New York, New York. 1992

I Can See You Naked, by Ron Hoff. Andrews and McMeel; New York, New York. 1992

Make Presentations With Confidence, by Vivian Buchan. Barrons Educational Series Inc.; New York, New York. 1997

New Dress for Success, by John T. Molloy. Warner Books; New York, New York. 1988.

Peace From Nervous Suffering, by Dr. Claire Weeks. Bantam Books; New York, New York. 1972.

Positive Imaging, by Dr. Norman Vincent Peale. Ballantine Books. 1996

Presentations Plus, by David Peoples. John Wiley & Sons; New York, New York. 1992

Stage Fright is a Villain, by Robert F. Moss. New York Times News Service; New York, New York. 1992

Stage Fright, Its Role in Acting, by Stephen Aaron. 1986.

The Book of Lists, by David Wallechinsky and Amy Wallace, Book News, Inc. Portland, Or. 1997

The Conquest of Fear, by Basil King. Doubleday, Publication: 1926

www.ingramcontent.com/pod-product-compliance
Lightning Source LLC
Chambersburg PA
CBHW030749180526
45163CB00003B/956